HOW TO DRAW MANGA

LEARN TO DRAW AWESOME MANGA CHARACTERS
A STEP BY STEP MANGA DRAWING BOOK FOR KIDS, TEENS, AND ADULTS

D1737116

SHINJUKU PRESS

★ ★ ★ ★ ★

THANK YOU FOR GETTING OUR BOOK!

IF YOU FIND THIS DRAWING BOOK FUN AND USEFUL, WE WOULD BE VERY GRATEFUL IF YOU POST A SHORT REVIEW ON AMAZON! YOUR SUPPORT DOES MAKE A DIFFERENCE, AND WE READ EVERY REVIEW PERSONALLY.

IF YOU WOULD LIKE TO LEAVE A REVIEW, JUST HEAD ON OVER TO THIS BOOK'S AMAZON PAGE AND CLICK "WRITE A CUSTOMER REVIEW."

THANK YOU FOR YOUR SUPPORT!

★ ★ ★ ★ ★

TABLE OF CONTENTS

INTRODUCTION

LEARNING HOW TO DRAW CAN BE
OVERWHELMING AND YOU MIGHT
FEEL LIKE YOU ARE STUCK OR NOT
MAKING ANY PROGRESS.

BUT REMEMBER TO JUST ENJOY
THE PROCESS. NOBODY STARTS
AS A GENIUS; WE ALL MUST START
AT SOME POINT. IT IS JUST
A MATTER OF WHO GETS TO
THEIR GOAL FIRST, BEFORE THE
OTHERS.

IN THIS BOOK, WE WILL GUIDE YOU
ON HOW YOU CAN GET STARTED
WITH DRAWING. PRACTICE WILL BE THE KEY, OUR FAVORITE ARTISTS ALSO
STARTED BY DRAWING STICK FIGURES, PRACTICED FOR YEARS AND HONED
THEIR SKILLS.

YOU CAN DO IT TOO!

WHAT YOU WILL NEED

THERE ARE TWO TYPES OF ART AND YOUR ITEMS WILL DEPEND ON WHAT TYPE YOU WANT TO MAKE.

TRADITIONAL ART

PAPER

PENCIL

ERASER

DIGITAL ART

DRAWING TABLET/COMPUTER

HOW TO DRAW FEMALE MANGA EYES

LET'S DRAW SOME MANGA EYES! REMEMBER THAT YOUR CHARACTER CAN SHOW SO MUCH EMOTION WITH THEIR EYES. THEY CAN BE HAPPY, SAD, ANGRY AND A LOT MORE.

DRAWING IS ALL ABOUT SHAPES! IN THIS CASE, WE WILL START WITH DRAWING A CIRCLE.

YOU CAN CHANGE THE SHAPE OF YOUR CIRCLE LATER ON, DEPENDING ON THE EYE EMOTION YOU ARE GOING FOR.

IT CAN BE A HALF CIRCLE, AN OBLONG OR EVEN A SMALL CIRCLE.

DEFINE THE UPPER AND LOWER PART OF THE EYES WITH CURVES AND ADD A FEW LASHES FOR A MORE DRAMATIC EFFECT.

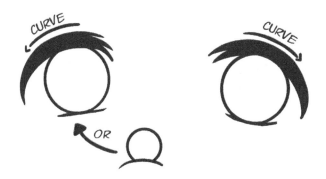

IDENTIFY WHERE YOUR CHARACTER IS LOOKING; PUT THE "IRIS" WHERE YOUR CHARACTER IS LOOKING AND ADD SOME EYE REFLECTIONS.

LET US LOOK AT MORE EYE SAMPLES WITH DIFFERENT EMOTIONS.

NOT A REALLY
HAPPY SMILE

HAPPY SMILE

CRYING

DISGUSTED

SHOCKED

MAD

HOW TO DRAW MALE MANGA EYES

LET'S DRAW SOME MALE MANGA EYES! REMEMBER THAT YOUR CHARACTERS CAN SHOW MANY DIFFERENT EMOTIONS WITH THEIR EYES. THEY CAN BE HAPPY, SAD, ANGRY, AND MUCH MORE.

KEEP IN MIND THAT THE MALE EYE IS RELATIVELY SMALLER AND SHARPER THAN A FEMALE'S EYE.

LET US AGAIN START WITH A CIRCLE.

ADD THE UPPER PART OF THE EYE. REMEMBER TO MAKE IT A SHARP CURVE SINCE THIS IS A MALE'S EYE. YOU'LL ALSO NOTICE THAT IT OVERLAPS WITH THE CIRCLE.

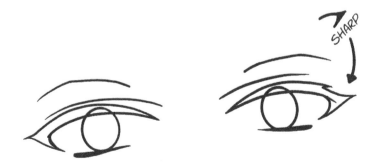

IDENTIFY WHERE YOUR CHARACTER IS LOOKING. PUT THE "IRIS" IN WHERE YOUR CHARACTER IS LOOKING AND ADD SOME EYE REFLECTIONS. YOU'LL ALSO NOTICE THAT I ALREADY SHADED THE UPPER PART OF THE EYE TO BETTER DEFINE IT.

LET US LOOK AT MORE EYE SAMPLES SHOWING DIFFERENT EMOTIONS.

NOT A REALLY HAPPY SMILE   HAPPY SMILE

CRYING   CRYING

SMIRKING   SMILING

HOW TO DRAW A MALE HEAD (FRONT VIEW)

LET'S DRAW SOME MANGA HEADS! WE LEARNED HOW TO DRAW THE EYES, NOW LET'S PUT THEM INSIDE THE HEAD!

START WITH A CIRCLE, THIS DOES NOT NEED TO BE A PERFECT CIRCLE.

PUT A VERTICAL GUIDE LINE IN THE MIDDLE OF THE CIRCLE.

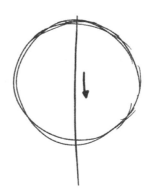

PUT A HORIZONTAL GUIDE LINE IN THE MIDDLE OF THE CIRCLE.

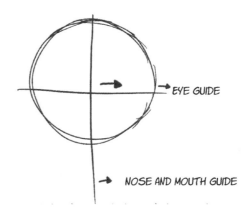

EYE GUIDE

NOSE AND MOUTH GUIDE

PUT ANOTHER HORIZONTAL
GUIDELINE BELOW THE CIRCLE;
THIS WILL DEFINE WHERE THE
CHEEKS WILL BE.

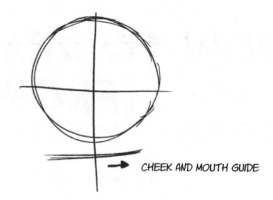

CHEEK AND MOUTH GUIDE

CONNECT THE CIRCLE TO THE
HORIZONTAL LINE BY USING A
DIAGONAL LINE

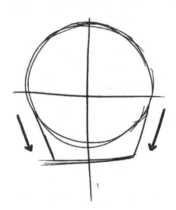

DO ANOTHER SET OF DIAGONAL
LINES AND CONNECT THEM THE
VERTICAL LINES. THIS WILL SERVE
AS THE CHIN.

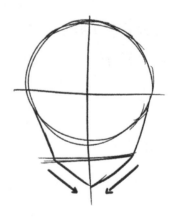

CREATE YOUR FINAL SKETCH
FOLLOWING THE GUIDES.
REMEMBER TO MAKE THE CURVES
SHARPER AS THIS IS A MALE'S
HEAD. FOLLOW THE GUIDELINES,
ADDING THE EYES WE DID
EARLIER AND PUTTING IN THE
NOSE AND MOUTH.

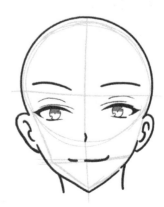

ADD THE HAIR. REMEMBER TO ADD THE HAIR SLIGHTLY ABOVE THE HEAD'S ARC GUIDE.

CLEAN UP THE LINES. NOW, YOU HAVE A MALE HEAD!

HOW TO DRAW A MALE HEAD (DIFFERENT ANGLES)

WE LEARNED HOW TO DRAW A MALE MANGA HEAD IN THE FRONT VIEW. NOW, LET US DRAW THE MALE HEAD FROM DIFFERENT ANGLES.

START WITH A CIRCLE, THIS DOES NOT NEED TO BE A PERFECT CIRCLE.

DO AN ARC BESIDE THE FIRST CIRCLE. THIS WILL SERVE AS THE BACK OF THE HEAD. THE BOTTOM OF THE FIRST CIRCLE WILL BE YOUR BASIS ON WHERE TO DRAW THE EYES.

PUT A VERTICAL GUIDE LINE IN YOUR FIRST CIRCLE; THIS WILL DEPEND ON HOW TILTED YOU WANT THE HEAD TO LOOK. THIS LINE WILL ALSO SERVE AS A GUIDE FOR THE EYES, NOSE, AND MOUTH.

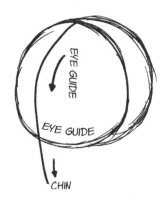

PUT ANOTHER HORIZONTAL
GUIDE LINE BELOW THE
CIRCLE; THIS WILL DEFINE
WHERE THE CHEEKS WILL BE.

CONNECT THE CIRCLE TO
THE VERTICAL LINE BY USING
DIAGONAL LINES. ADD AN
OBLONG AS A GUIDE FOR THE
EAR.

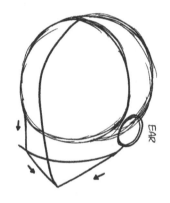

START DOING THE SKETCH BY
FOLLOWING THE GUIDELINES,
DO NOT FORGET TO MAKE
THE CURVES SHARPER.

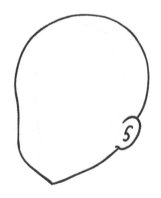

LET US ADD THE EYES, NOSE,
AND MOUTH BY FOLLOWING
THE GUIDELINES I MENTIONED
EARLIER.

NOW, ADD THE HAIR. REMEMBER THAT THE TOP OF THE HAIRLINE IS SLIGHTLY ABOVE YOUR HEAD GUIDE.

CLEAN EVERYTHING AND NOW YOU HAVE YOUR HEAD TILTED IN 3/4 VIEW.

HOW TO DRAW A MALE HEAD (SIDE VIEW)

WE LEARNED HOW TO DRAW A MALE MANGA HEAD IN FRONT VIEW. NOW, LET US DRAW THE MALE HEAD IN DIFFERENT ANGLES.

START WITH AN ELLIPSE; THIS DOES NOT NEED TO BE PERFECT.

PUT A VERTICAL AND HORIZONTAL LINE IN THE MIDDLE OF THE ELLIPSE. ON THE LOWER HALF OF THE ELLIPSE, ADD ANOTHER HORIZONTAL LINE IN THE MIDDLE. LAST HORIZONTAL LINE WILL BE DIRECTLY BELOW THE ELLIPSE.

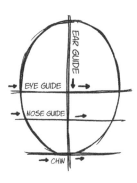

DRAW A CIRCLE INSIDE THE ELLIPSE. THEN CONNECT THE GUIDELINES USING DIAGONAL LINES.

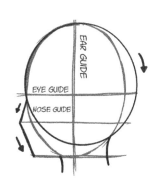

START DOING THE SKETCH
FOLLOWING THE GUIDELINES.
DO NOT FORGET TO MAKE
THE CURVES SHARPER!

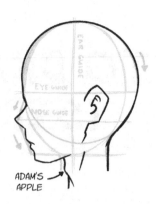

CLEAN UP THE SKETCH.

ADD THE HAIR, AND NOW YOU HAVE
A MALE HEAD IN THE SIDE VIEW.

MORE HEAD ANGLES.

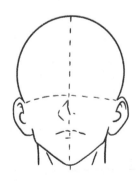 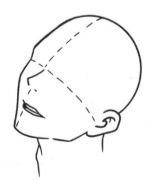 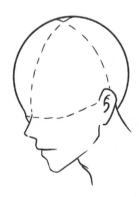

HOW TO DRAW A FEMALE HEAD (FRONT VIEW)

LET'S DRAW SOME FEMALE MANGA HEADS! WE LEARNED HOW TO DRAW THE EYES, NOW LET'S PUT THEM INSIDE THE HEAD!

START WITH A CIRCLE, THIS DOES NOT NEED TO BE A PERFECT CIRCLE.

PUT A VERTICAL GUIDE LINE IN THE MIDDLE OF THE CIRCLE.

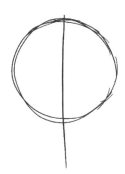

PUT A HORIZONTAL GUIDE LINE IN THE MIDDLE OF THE CIRCLE.

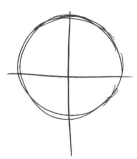

PUT ANOTHER HORIZONTAL GUIDE LINE BELOW THE CIRCLE; THIS WILL DEFINE WHERE THE CHEEKS WILL BE.

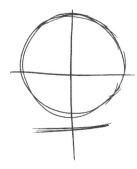

CONNECT THE CIRCLE TO
THE HORIZONTAL LINE BY
USING A DIAGONAL LINE.

DO ANOTHER SET OF
DIAGONAL LINES AND
CONNECT THEM TO THE
VERTICAL LINES. THIS WILL
SERVE AS THE CHIN.

CREATE YOUR FINAL
SKETCH FOLLOWING THE
GUIDES. REMEMBER TO
MAKE SOME CURVES FOR
THE CHEEKS.

CLEAN UP THE LINES. YOU
NOW HAVE A FEMALE MANGA
HEAD.

I ADDED THE EYES WE DID
EARLIER AND INCLUDED A
NOSE, MOUTH, AND HAIR.

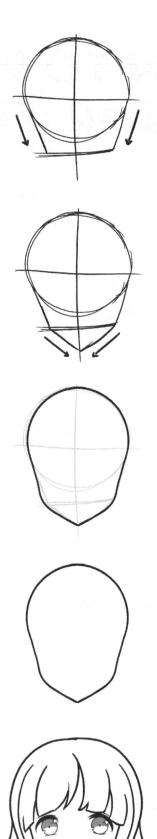

16

HOW TO DRAW A FEMALE HEAD (DIFFERENT ANGLES)

WE LEARNED HOW TO DRAW A FEMALE MANGA HEAD IN A FRONT VIEW. NOW, LET US DRAW THE FEMALE HEAD AT DIFFERENT ANGLES.

START WITH A CIRCLE; THIS DOES NOT NEED TO BE A PERFECT CIRCLE.

DO AN ARC BESIDE THE FIRST CIRCLE. THIS WILL SERVE AS THE BACK OF THE HEAD. THE BOTTOM OF THE FIRST CIRCLE WILL BE YOUR BASIS ON WHERE TO DRAW THE EYES.

PUT A VERTICAL GUIDE LINE IN YOUR FIRST CIRCLE; THIS WILL DEPEND ON HOW TILTED YOU WANT THE HEAD TO LOOK. THIS LINE WILL ALSO SERVE AS A GUIDE FOR THE EYES, NOSE, AND MOUTH.

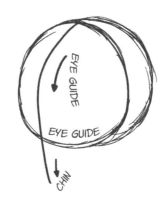

PUT ANOTHER HORIZONTAL
GUIDE LINE BELOW THE CIRCLE;
THIS WILL DEFINE WHERE THE
CHEEKS WILL BE.

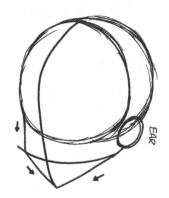

CONNECT THE CIRCLE TO
THE VERTICAL LINE BY USING
DIAGONAL LINES.
ADD AN OBLONG AS A GUIDE FOR
THE EAR.

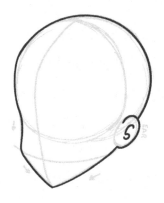

START DOING THE
SKETCH BY FOLLOWING
THE GUIDELINES; DO NOT
FORGET TO EXAGGERATE
THE CURVES.

LET US ADD THE EYES,
NOSE, AND MOUTH BY
FOLLOWING THE GUIDELINES
I MENTIONED EARLIER.

NOW, ADD THE HAIR. REMEMBER THAT THE TOP OF THE HAIRLINE IS SLIGHTLY ABOVE YOUR HEAD GUIDE.

CLEAN UP EVERYTHING AND NOW YOU HAVE YOUR HEAD TILTED IN A ³/₄ VIEW.

HOW TO DRAW A FEMALE HEAD (SIDE VIEW)

WE LEARNED HOW TO DRAW A FEMALE MANGA HEAD IN THE FRONT VIEW. NOW, LET US DRAW THE FEMALE HEAD FROM DIFFERENT ANGLES.

START WITH AN ELLIPSE; THIS DOES NOT NEED TO BE PERFECT.

MAKE A VERTICAL AND HORIZONTAL LINE IN THE MIDDLE OF THE ELLIPSE. ON THE LOWER HALF OF THE ELLIPSE ADD ANOTHER HORIZONTAL LINE IN THE MIDDLE. THE LAST HORIZONTAL LINE WILL BE DIRECTLY BELOW THE ELLIPSE.

DRAW A CIRCLE INSIDE THE ELLIPSE. THEN CONNECT THE GUIDELINES USING DIAGONAL LINES.

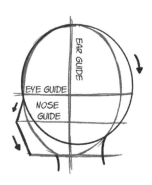

START DOING THE
SKETCH FOLLOWING
THE GUIDELINES. DO NOT
FORGET TO EXAGGERATE
THE CURVES.

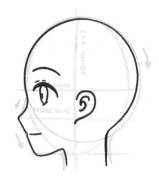

CLEAN UP THE SKETCH.

ADD THE HAIR AND NOW
YOU HAVE A FEMALE
HEAD IN SIDE VIEW.

MORE HEAD ANGLES.

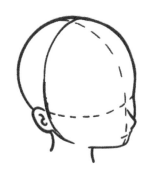 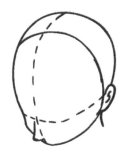 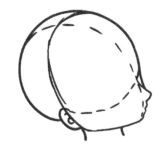

HOW TO DRAW A MANGA MOUTH

ASIDE FROM USING THE EYES AND EYEBROWS, THE MOUTH CAN ALSO CONVEY MANY EXPRESSIONS AND GIVE MORE LIFE TO OUR CHARACTER.

ARE YOU WONDERING WHERE YOU SHOULD PLACE THE MOUTH? THERE'S NO NEED TO WORRY. IF YOU FOLLOWED THE GUIDES ON HOW WE DREW THE HEADS, YOU WILL SEE GUIDES FOR WHERE TO PLACE THE MOUTH AS SEEN IN THE PICTURES BELOW.

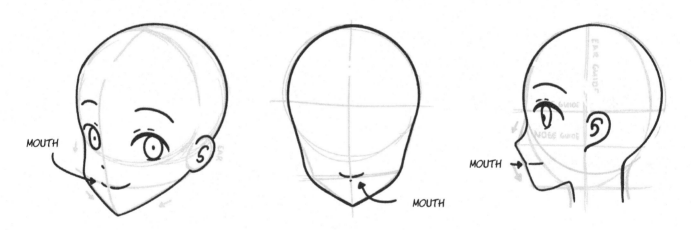

LET'S TRY DRAWING DIFFERENT KINDS OF MOUTHS.

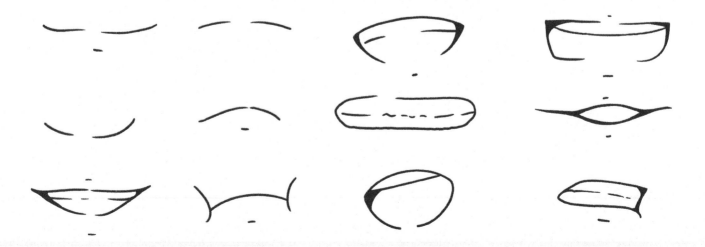

22

IF YOU ARE HAVING A HARD TIME DRAWING OR IMAGINING THE MOUTH YOU WANT, TRY LOOKING AT REAL-LIFE PHOTOS OR MAKING THE MOUTH EXPRESSION THAT YOU WANT TO DRAW.

YOU CAN ALSO CREATE EXAGGERATED MOUTH EXPRESSIONS TO CONVEY MORE EXTREME FEELINGS.

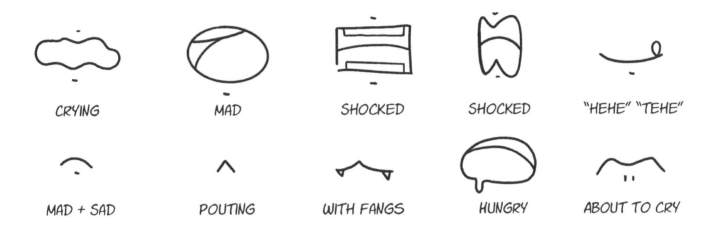

CRYING   MAD   SHOCKED   SHOCKED   "HEHE" "TEHE"

MAD + SAD   POUTING   WITH FANGS   HUNGRY   ABOUT TO CRY

HOW TO DRAW FEMALE HAIR

LET US NOW LEARN HOW TO DO SOME HAIR AND GIVE LIFE TO OUR CHARACTER.

REMEMBER HOW WE DREW THE HEAD? TAKE A LOOK AT THESE 3 FEMALE HEADS WE DREW FROM THE EARLIER LESSONS. THE HAIR WILL GO A LITTLE A BIT ABOVE THEIR ACTUAL SKULL.

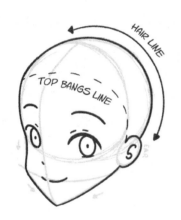 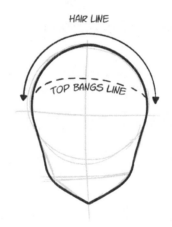 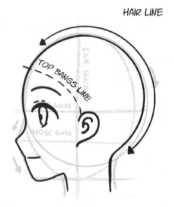

LET US PRACTICE DRAWING SOME HAIR! HAIR SHOULD BE "FLOWY" AND FOLLOW THE CHARACTER'S MOVEMENT BUT FOR NOW, LET US DO SOME "STILL" OR "NOT MOVING" HAIR FIRST.

DRAW THE HEAD.

ADD THE HAIR.

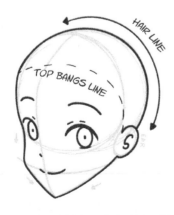 

ADD DETAILS TO THE HAIR. YOU CAN MAKE SOME LINES THICKER TO GIVE IT MORE DEPTH. YOU CAN ALSO ADD ADDITIONAL STRANDS TO GIVE THE HAIR MORE VOLUME.

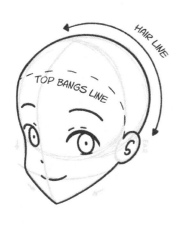

LET'S DRAW SOME MORE HAIR AND THIS TIME, LET'S MAKE IT MORE "FLOWY."

THINK OF HOW YOU WANT YOUR HAIR TO MOVE. IN THIS EXAMPLE, WE'LL MAKE THE HAIR FLOW FROM LEFT TO RIGHT.

FOLLOW THE FLOW YOU
DECIDED ON AS YOU DRAW
YOUR STRANDS OF HAIR.
REMEMBER TO MAKE LONG
CURVED LINES, RATHER THAN
DRAWING SHORT STRAIGHT
LINES AS DOING SO CAN MAKE
THE HAIR LOOK STIFF.

WIND FLOW

ADD SOME STRANDS OF HAIR
AND MAKE SOME LINES THICKER.
REMEMBER TO ALWAYS
FOLLOW THE "FLOW," IN THIS
CASE, IT IS LEFT TO RIGHT.

ALWAYS KEEP IN MIND THAT THE HAIR IS SOFT AND YOU CAN BEND IT
HOWEVER YOU WANT.

HOW TO DRAW
FEMALE HAIR TYPES

AFTER LEARNING HOW TO MAKE THE HAIR FOLLOW HER MOVEMENTS, LET US STUDY DIFFERENT HAIR TYPES AND STYLES.

STRAIGHT WAVY CURLY CURLY

BRAIDED TWIN TAILED BUN BUN PIXIE SHORT

HOW TO DRAW BRAIDS AND CURLY HAIR.

START WITH SOME HEART-LIKE SHAPES, THEN ADD A BIT OF DRAMATIC HAIR STRAND DETAILS. THERE IS NO SPECIFIC PATTERN ON HOW YOU SHOULD ADD THE STRANDS. JUST PUT THEM WHERE YOU FEEL LIKE.

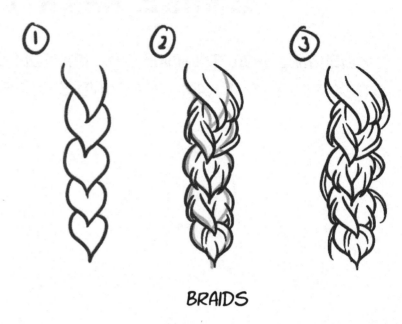

BRAIDS

START WITH SOME CURVED-RECTANGULAR SHAPES THEN ADD A BIT OF DRAMA WITH THE HAIR STRAND DETAILS. THERE'S NO SPECIFIC PATTERN TO HOW YOU SHOULD ADD THE STRANDS, JUST PUT THEM WHERE YOU FEEL LIKE.

CURLS

HOW TO DRAW MALE HAIR

LET US NOW LEARN HOW TO DRAW SOME MALE HAIR AND GIVE LIFE TO OUR CHARACTER.

REMEMBER HOW WE DREW THE HEAD? TAKE A LOOK AT THESE 3 MALE HEADS WE DREW FROM THE EARLIER LESSONS. THE HAIR WILL GO A LITTLE BIT ABOVE THEIR ACTUAL "SKULL."

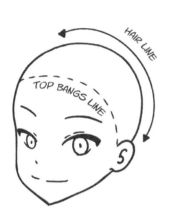 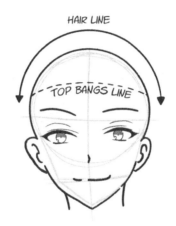 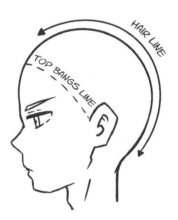

LET US PRACTICE DRAWING SOME MORE HAIR! HAIR SHOULD BE "FLOWY" AND FOLLOW THE CHARACTER'S MOVEMENT BUT FIRST, LET US DO SOME "STILL" OR "NOT MOVING" HAIR.

DRAW THE HEAD.   ADD THE HAIR.

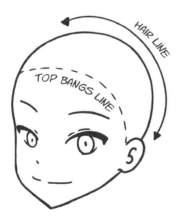 

ADD DETAILS TO THE HAIR. YOU
CAN MAKE SOME LINES THICKER
TO GIVE IT MORE DEPTH. YOU
CAN ALSO ADD ADDITIONAL
STRANDS TO GIVE THE HAIR
MORE VOLUME.

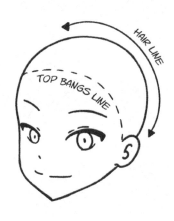

LET'S DRAW SOME MORE HAIR AND THIS TIME, LET US MAKE IT MORE
"FLOWY."

THINK OF HOW YOU WANT YOUR
HAIR TO MOVE. IN THIS EXAMPLE,
WE'LL MAKE THE HAIR FLOW FROM
LEFT TO RIGHT.

FOLLOW THE FLOW YOU DECIDED
ON AS YOU DRAW YOUR HAIR
STRANDS. REMEMBER TO MAKE
LONG CURVED LINES RATHER THAN
DRAWING SHORT STRAIGHT LINES,
AS DOING SO CAN MAKE YOUR HAIR
LOOK STIFF.

ADD SOME HAIR STRANDS
AND MAKE SOME HAIR LINES
THICKER. REMEMBER TO
ALWAYS FOLLOW THE
"FLOW," IN THIS CASE,
LEFT TO RIGHT.

WIND FLOW

ALWAYS KEEP IN MIND THAT THE HAIR IS SOFT AND IT CAN BEND HOWEVER
YOU WANT.

HOW TO DRAW EXPRESSIONS (FEMALE)

LET US NOW MAKE DIFFERENT EXPRESSIONS AND USE ALL THAT WE LEARNED ABOUT HOW TO DRAW THE HEAD, EYES AND MOUTH!

A HAPPY EXPRESSION. NOTICE THAT I USED THE EYES THAT WE DREW DURING THE EYE TUTORIAL AND JUST ADDED THE MOUTH TO GIVE MORE LIFE TO THE CHARACTER'S EXPRESSION.

YOU CAN ALSO INCLUDE SOME HAIR FLOW AND MOVEMENT, LIKE THE SAMPLE WHERE OUR CHARACTER IS SO HAPPY THAT SHE LOOKS LIKE SHE JUMPED OUT OF HAPPINESS AND EXCITEMENT.

A MAD/ANGRY EXPRESSION. YOU CAN ALSO USE HEAD ANGLES. YOU CAN PLAY WITH HOW YOU WANT YOUR HEAD TO FACE OR LOOK.

NOTICE HERE THAT THE HEAD IS KIND OF LOOKING DOWN, BUT AT THE SAME TIME, THE EYES ARE STILL LOOKING STRAIGHT AHEAD.

HERE ARE SOME ADDITIONAL EXPRESSIONS THAT YOU CAN TRY TO DO.

SAD / CRYING.   SHOCKED / SURPRISED

ONE THING TO REMEMBER ABOUT DRAWING SHOCKED / SURPRISED
EXPRESSIONS IS THAT THE PUPILS OF THE EYE ARE SMALLER.

EMBARRASSED

REMEMBER THAT YOU CAN DO EXAGGERATED EXPRESSIONS IN MANGA ART.

HOW TO DRAW EXPRESSIONS (MALE)

NOW, LET US DRAW DIFFERENT EXPRESSIONS USING ALL THAT WE LEARNED ABOUT HOW TO DRAW THE HEAD, EYES AND MOUTH!

A HAPPY EXPRESSION. NOTICE I HAVE USED THE EYES THAT WE DREW DURING THE EYE TUTORIAL AND JUST ADDED THE MOUTH TO GIVE MORE LIFE TO THE CHARACTER'S EXPRESSION.

YOU CAN ALSO INCLUDE SOME HAIR FLOW AND MOVEMENT, AS IN THE SAMPLE WHERE OUR CHARACTER IS EXTREMELY HAPPY AND LOOKS LIKE HE JUMPED OUT OF HAPPINESS AND EXCITEMENT.

A SMIRKING EXPRESSION. YOU CAN PLAY WITH THE HEAD ANGLE. NOTICE HERE THAT THE HEAD IS SOMEWHAT TILTED.

ALSO, THE EYES I USED HERE ARE FROM THE EYE TUTORIAL LESSON. PARTNERING IT WITH A SMIRKING MOUTH GIVES THE CHARACTER A MUCH MORE EXPRESSIVE LOOK.

HERE ARE SOME ADDITIONAL EXPRESSIONS THAT YOU CAN TRY TO DO.

SAD/CRYING

SHOCKED / SURPRISED

ONE THING TO REMEMBER ABOUT DRAWING SHOCKED OR SURPRISED EXPRESSIONS IS THAT THE "PUPILS" OF THE EYE ARE SMALLER.

EMBARRASSED

NOTE: REMEMBER THAT YOU CAN DO EXAGGERATED EXPRESSIONS IN MANGA ART.

LET US DO SOME EXAGGERATED EXPRESSIONS!

EXTREMELY EMBARRASSED

YOU CAN CHANGE THE FACE SHAPE, EYES AND MOUTH TO PORTRAY MORE EXTREME EMOTIONS.

YOU CAN ALSO ADD ELEMENTS LIKE TEARS (TO MAKE THE CHARACTER LOOK LIKE SHE IS ABOUT TO CRY BECAUSE OF EMBARRASSMENT)

THIS ALSO WORKS WITH MALE CHARACTERS.

DO NOT BE AFRAID TO EXPERIMENT WITH LOTS OF DIFFERENT EXPRESSIONS.

WORRIED　　　SHOCKED + AMAZED　　　WAILING (CRYING)

WAILING (CRYING)   SHOCKED FACES

NOTICE THAT BOTH ARE SHOWING A SHOCKED EXPRESSION, BUT THE
SECOND ONE IS MORE EXTREME! REMEMBER, YOU CAN SIMPLIFY THE
SHAPES LIKE WHAT I DID TO THE FACE OF THE SECOND ONE; HIS
SIMPLIFIED FACE MADE HIM LOOK MORE SHOCKED THAN THE FIRST
ONE. YOU CAN ALSO USE THE HAIR TO GIVE MORE DEPTH TO THEIR
EXPRESSIONS, AS IN THE SAMPLES ABOVE. THE HAIR IS ALSO GOING
STRAIGHT UP, SHOWING THAT THEY ARE SHOCKED.

HOW TO DRAW A MANGA BODY

FINALLY, LET US LEARN HOW TO DRAW A CHARACTER'S BODY!
THIS LESSON WILL BE DIVIDED INTO FIVE (5) DIFFERENT PARTS.
(1) HOW TO DRAW THE HEAD
(2) HOW TO DRAW THE TORSO
(3) HOW TO DRAW THE ARMS AND HANDS
(4) HOW TO DRAW THE LEGS
(5) HOW TO CONNECT THEM ALL IN ONE DRAWING

LEARNING AND MASTERING EACH PART WILL MAKE IT EASIER FOR YOU TO DRAW DIFFERENT POSES.

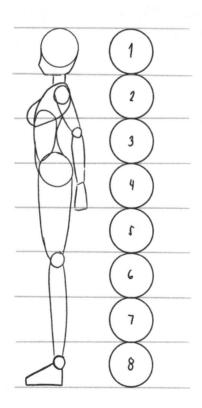

A NORMAL BODY'S TOTAL HEIGHT IS EIGHT (8) HEADS.

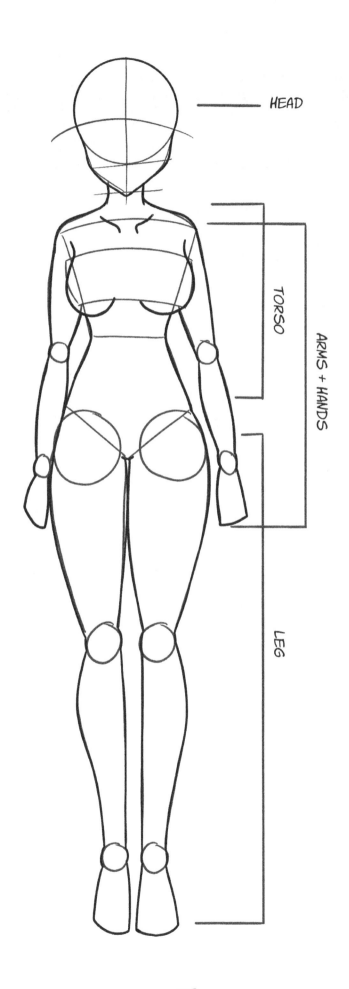

HEAD

TORSO

ARMS + HANDS

LEG

39

THE FEMALE TORSO

START WITH DRAWING THE BASIC SHAPES THAT YOU WILL NEED FOR THE TORSO.

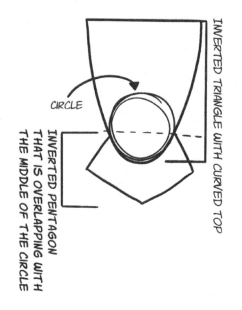

CIRCLE

INVERTED PENTAGON THAT IS OVERLAPPING WITH THE MIDDLE OF THE CIRCLE

INVERTED TRIANGLE WITH CURVED TOP

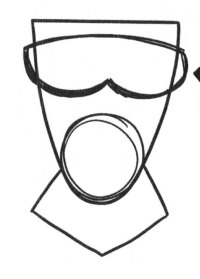

ADD THE BREAST GUDIE. YOU CAN MAKE THIS BIGGER OR SMALLER DEPENDING ON THE BREAST TYPE THAT YOU WANT TO MAKE

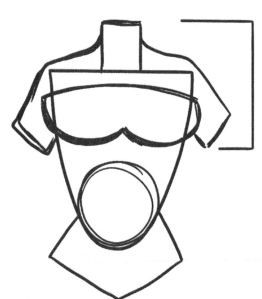

NECK, SHOULDER AND ARM GUIDE. YOU CAN POSITION THE ARM IN ANY WAY JUST REMEMBER HOW IT CONNECTS WITH THE TORSO.

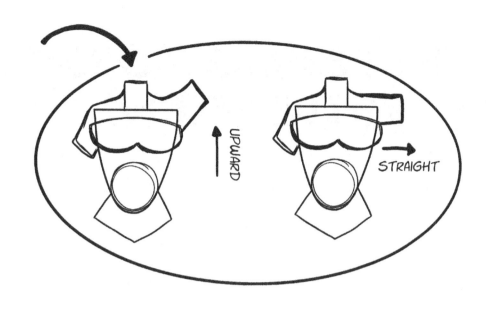

UPWARD

STRAIGHT

START TRACING YOUR GUIDE.

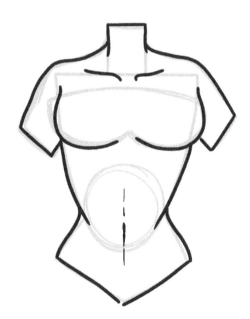

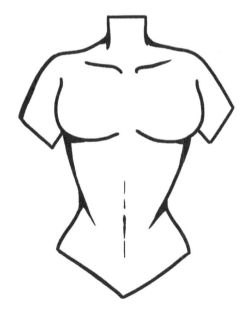

DO NOT FORGET TO
MAKE EXAGGERATED
CURVE LINES TO
EMPHASIZE THE BREAST
AND WAIST.

CLEAN YOUR SKETCH AND
FINALIZE YOUR LINES.

THE FEMALE TORSO
(SIDE VIEW)

START WITH A WEIRD BEAN SHAPE WITH A SLIGHTLY DIAGONAL LINE ON TOP.

YOU CAN ALSO START BY DRAWING TWO CIRCLES WITH A CURVED LINE THAT CONNECTS THEM.

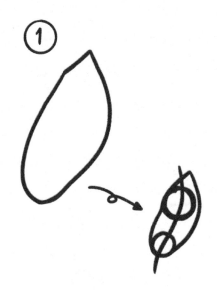

NEXT, ADD THE GUIDE FOR THE BREAST AREA. YOU CAN ADJUST ITS SIZE BASED ON HOW SMALL OR BIG YOU WANT THE BREAST.

ALSO ADD THE WAIST GUIDELINES. THIS WILL LOOK LIKE A TRIANGLE WITH A SEPARATED TIP.

TRACE YOUR GUIDELINES, DO NOT FORGET TO EXAGGERATE THE BODY CURVES.

CLEAN YOUR LINES AND YOU ARE NOW DONE!

TRY TO CONNECT THIS WITH THE SIDE VIEW HEAD WE DID IN THE EARLIER LESSON.

THE FEMALE TORSO
(BACK VIEW)

① START WITH AN INVERTED
TRIANGLE WITH A CURVED END.

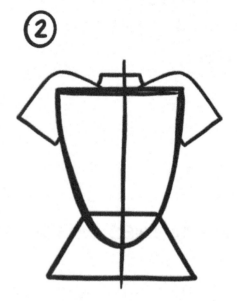

② ADD THE GUIDE FOR THE
ARMS, NECK AND WAIST.

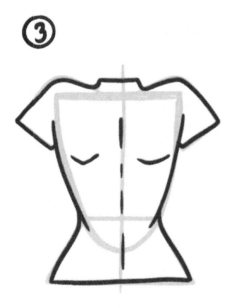

③ TRACE YOUR GUIDELINES
AND REMEMBER TO USE
EXAGGERATED CURVES.

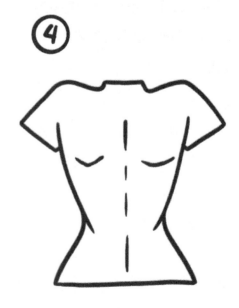

④ CLEAN YOUR LINES AND NOW
YOU'LL HAVE THE BACK TORSO!

THE MALE TORSO
(FRONT VIEW)

START WITH A STRAIGHT
LINE AND ADD YOUR
BREAST GUIDE. THIS WILL
LOOK LIKE A WEIRDLY
SHAPED OCTAGON.

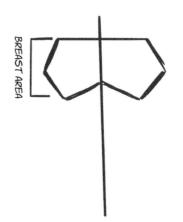

ADD THE SHAPE GUIDES
FOR THE STOMACH AND AN
ARC FOR THE WAIST GUIDE.

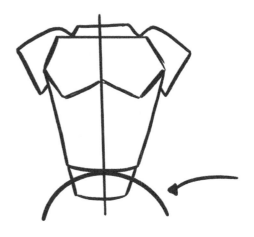

START TRACING YOUR GUIDELINES.
TAKE NOTE THAT, UNLIKE THE FEMALE
BODY, THE MALE BODY TENDS TO BE
BULKY AND COMES WITH A LOT OF
SOMEWHAT STRAIGHT LINES INSTEAD
OF EXAGGERATED CURVES.

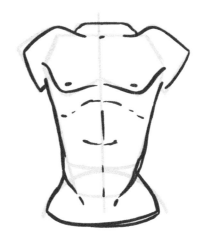

CLEAN UP YOUR LINES. NOW,
YOU HAVE A MALE TORSO!
TRY CONNECTING THIS TO THE
MALE HEAD WE DID IN EARLIER
LESSONS.

LET'S DO ANOTHER ONE!

SIDE VIEW

START WITH DRAWING
YOUR SHAPE GUIDES.

TRACE YOUR GUIDES.
REMEMBER THAT
THE MALE BODY IS
BULKY, UNLIKE THE
FEMALE BODY.

CLEAN UP YOUR LINES.
TRY TO CONNECT
THIS INTO THE MALE
HEAD WE DID IN THE
PREVIOUS LESSONS.

THE FEMALE ARMS

FIRST, LET US DEFINE THE SHAPES THAT WE WILL BE USING TO CREATE A FEMALE ARM!

NOTE: THE CIRCLE WILL BE USED TO CONNECT THE ARM TO THE TORSO WE DID IN THE PREVIOUS LESSON.

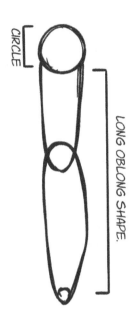

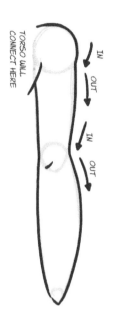

TRACE YOUR GUIDELINES, DO NOT FORGET TO MAKE EXAGGERATED CURVES AS USUAL!

TAKE NOTE OF THE ARROWS I PUT HERE, REMEMBER THAT THE FEMALE ARM DOES NOT JUST GO IN A STRAIGHT LINE. IT GOES IN AND OUT AND IN AGAIN.

CLEAN UP YOUR LINES AND YOU ARE DONE! TRY CONNECTING THIS TO THE FEMALE TORSO WE DREW EARLIER

LET'S TRY ANOTHER ONE DOING A DIFFERENT POSE.

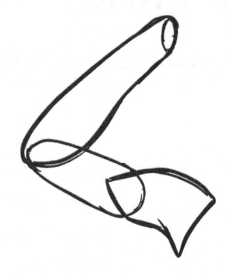

FIRST, THINK OF A POSE YOU CAN DO AND START DEFINING AND PLACING THE SHAPES FOLLOWING THE POSE THAT YOU WANT TO DRAW.

START TRACING YOUR GUIDELINES. TAKE NOTE OF THE PART WITH THE ARROW; IT GOES IN FRONT OF THE OTHER LINE.

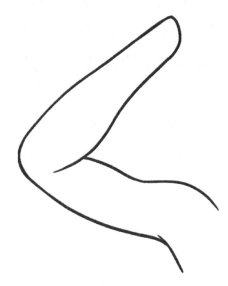

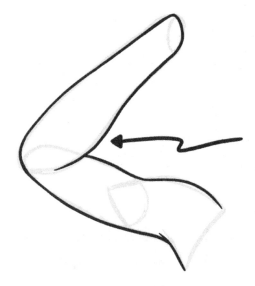

CLEAN YOUR LINES AND NOW, YOU HAVE YOUR ARMS! TRY TO CONNECT THEM WITH THE TORSO.

BONUS!
CONNECT BOTH ARMS WE DID TO THE TORSO!

THE FEMALE LEGS

LET'S IDENTIFY
THE SHAPES THAT
WE WILL NEED TO
DRAW THE LEGS.

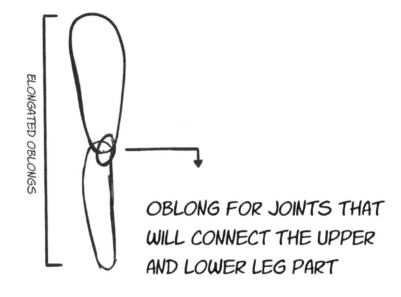

ELONGATED OBLONGS

OBLONG FOR JOINTS THAT
WILL CONNECT THE UPPER
AND LOWER LEG PART

START
TRACING YOUR
GUIDELINES.
NOTICE THE
ARROWS THAT
I SHOW GOING
OUT AND IN AND
OUT. REMEMBER
TO MAKE
EXAGGERATED
CURVES.

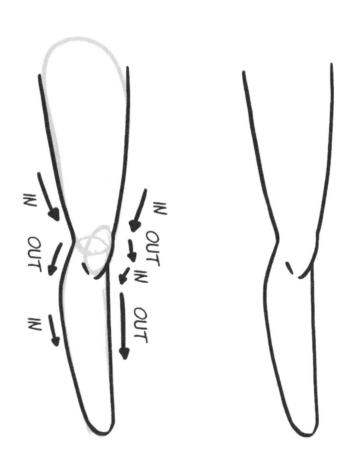

CLEAN UP
YOUR LINES!
NOW, YOU
HAVE YOUR
FEMALE LEGS.

LET'S DO ANOTHER ONE – THE SIDE VIEW.

START
BY DOING
YOUR
SHAPE
GUIDES.

TRACE YOUR
GUIDES. TAKE
NOTE OF
THE ARROWS
GOING IN AND
OUT.

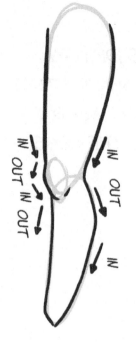

CLEAN
UP YOUR
LINES!
NOW, YOU
HAVE
YOUR
FEMALE
LEGS.

TRY CONNECTING THE
LEGS TO THE TORSO!
NOW WE ALMOST HAVE
A CHARACTER WITH A
WHOLE BODY!

THE MALE ARMS

LET US FIRST DEFINE THE SHAPES WE WILL USE TO CREATE A MALE ARM!

NOTE: THE OBLONG WILL BE USED TO CONNECT THE ARM INTO THE TORSO WE DREW IN THE PREVIOUS LESSON.

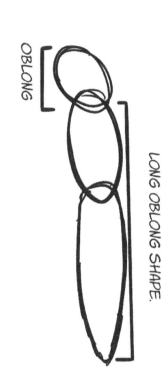

TRACE YOUR GUIDELINES; REMEMBER THAT THE MALE BODY IS MORE BULKY RATHER THAN CURVY.

YOU CAN PLAY WITH THE MUSCLES AND MAKE THEM SMALLER OR BIGGER, DEPENDING ON THE CHARACTER THAT YOU ARE GOING FOR.

CLEAN UP YOUR LINES AND YOU ARE DONE! TRY CONNECTING THIS TO THE MALE TORSO WE DID EARLIER.

LET'S TRY ANOTHER ONE DOING A DIFFERENT POSE.

 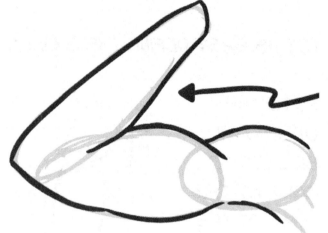

FIRST, THINK OF A POSE THAT YOU WANT TO DO AND START DEFINING AND PLACING THE SHAPES FOLLOWING THE POSE THAT YOU WANT TO DRAW.

START TRACING YOUR GUIDELINES. TAKE NOTE OF THE PART WITH THE ARROW, IT GOES IN FRONT OF THE OTHER LINE.

CLEAN UP YOUR LINES AND NOW YOU HAVE YOUR ARMS! TRY TO CONNECT THEM TO THE TORSO!

BONUS!
CONNECT BOTH ARMS THAT WE DID WITH THE TORSO!

THE MALE LEGS

LET US IDENTIFY THE SHAPES THAT WE WILL NEED TO DRAW THE LEGS.

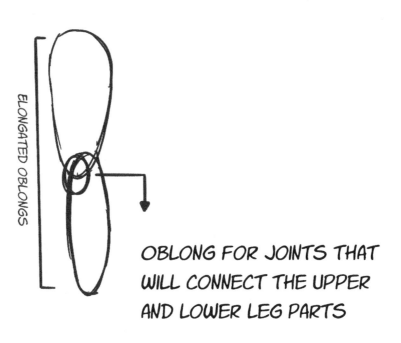

ELONGATED OBLONGS

OBLONG FOR JOINTS THAT WILL CONNECT THE UPPER AND LOWER LEG PARTS

START TRACING YOUR GUIDELINES. NOTICE THE ARROWS I DID GOING OUT AND IN AND OUT. REMEMBER THAT THE MALE BODY IS BULKY, NOT TOO CURVY.

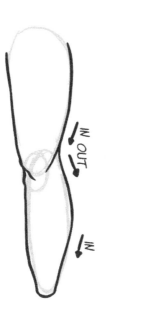

CLEAN YOUR LINES! NOW, YOU HAVE YOUR MALE LEGS.

LET'S DO ANOTHER ONE! – THE FLEXED VIEW.

START WITH
DOING YOUR
SHAPE
GUIDES.

TRACE YOUR
GUIDES.

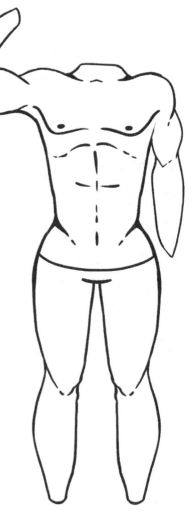

CLEAN UP YOUR LINES!
NOW, YOU HAVE YOUR
MALE LEGS.

TRY CONNECTING
THE LEGS TO
THE TORSO! NOW
WE ALMOST HAVE
A WHOLE BODY
CHARACTER!

ARMS AND HANDS

DRAWING IS ALL ABOUT SHAPES, SHAPES, AND MORE SHAPES!

THIS TIME WE WILL LEARN HOW TO DRAW THE FEMALE ARMS AND HANDS.

THESE SHAPES WILL BE YOUR BEST FRIEND IN THIS COURSE.

CIRCLES,
RECTANGLES,
TRIANGLES,
AND BOXES.

START WITH THINKING
WHAT YOU WANT THE
ARMS TO LOOK LIKE.
THEN PLACE THE
SHAPES ACCORDINGLY.

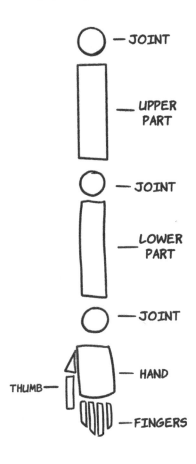

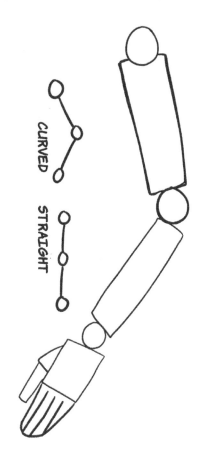

TRACE YOUR GUIDELINES AND REMEMBER TO PUT IN SOME EXAGGERATED CURVES. TAKE NOTE OF WHERE THE JOINTS ARE.

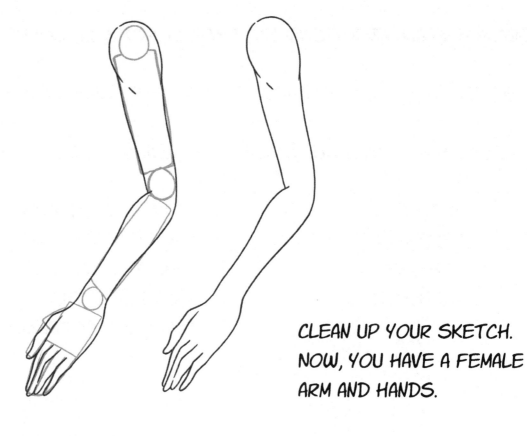

CLEAN UP YOUR SKETCH. NOW, YOU HAVE A FEMALE ARM AND HANDS.

MORE ABOUT DRAWING THE HANDS.

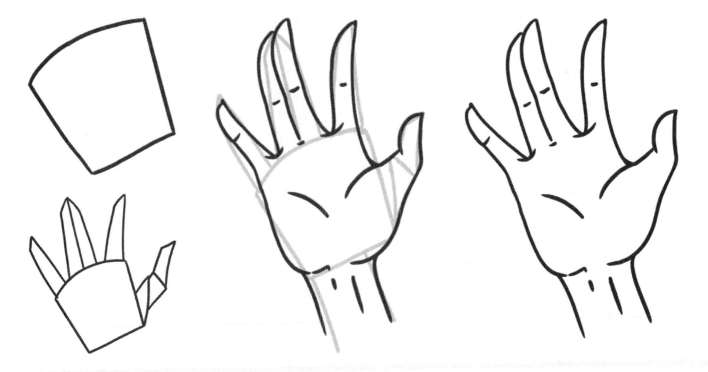

HOW TO DRAW BODY PROPORTIONS

LET US LEARN ABOUT BODY PROPORTIONS!

WE LEARNED HOW TO DO THE BODY PARTS. NOW LET US LEARN ABOUT BODY PROPORTIONS! HOW LONG SHOULD THE ARMS AND LEGS BE? REMEMBER THAT A FULL BODY CHARACTER IS 8 HEADS IN TOTAL.

REMEMBER THAT YOU CAN ALWAYS PLAY WITH PROPORTION; IT IS NOT ABSOLUTE. THIS GUIDE JUST AIMS TO HELP YOU FIND YOUR WAY TO START DRAWING.

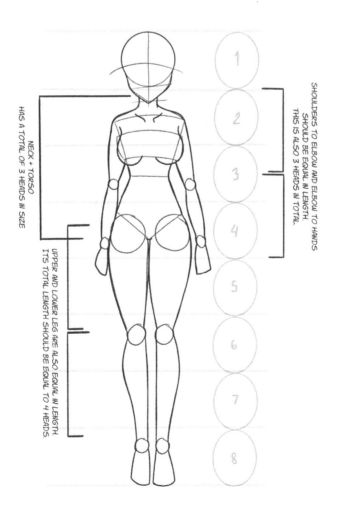

DIFFERENT BODY POSES

NOW THAT WE KNOW HOW TO DRAW THE BASIC BODY PARTS AND
PROPORTIONS, LET US TRY TO DRAW DIFFERENT BODY POSES AND
ACTION POSES.

TO START WITH, LOOK FOR A REFERENCE PHOTO THE POSE YOU WANT
TO DRAW. WITH THAT POSE IN MIND, TRY TO FIND THE "LINE OF ACTION," AN
IMAGINARY LINE THAT DEFINES HOW THE CHARACTER IS MOVING.

1. TAKE A LOOK AT THESE TWO POSES AND THINK OF THEM AS PHOTOS
OF REAL PEOPLE. SEE HOW THE "LINE OF ACTION" IS DEFINED. THE LINE
OF ACTION IS WHAT YOU WILL FOLLOW WHEN YOU PLOT THE SHAPES AND
GUIDES YOU WHEN YOU START DRAWING.

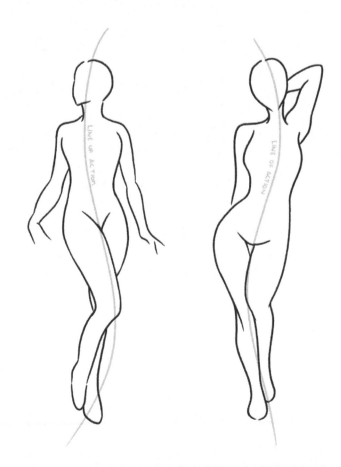

2. ONCE YOU HAVE DEFINED THE LINE OF ACTION, YOU CAN START DRAWING IN THE SHAPES AND GUIDES AS WE DID IN THE PREVIOUS LESSONS.

PLACE THE SHAPES BY FOLLOWING THE "LINE OF ACTION.

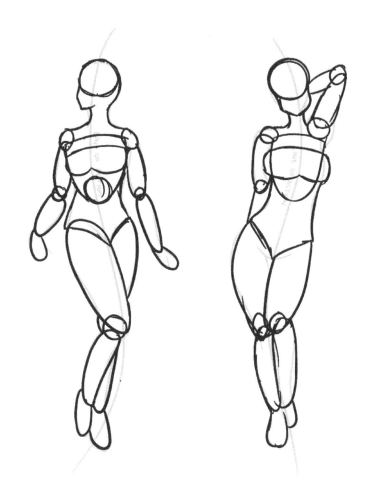

IF YOU ARE HAVING TROUBLE FINDING OR IDENTIFYING WHERE THE "LINE OF ACTION" GOES, DON'T WORRY! FIND LOTS OF REFERENCE PHOTOS AND LOOK AT THEM. PRACTICE WILL BE THE KEY! THE LINE OF ACTION CAN BE WHATEVER YOU FEEL IS RIGHT. THERE IS NO STANDARD AND DEFINITE RULE FOR HOW IT IS DONE.

MORE ABOUT LINE OF ACTION (MALE)

1. LOOK FOR A REFERENCE PHOTO.

2. TRY TO FIND THE LINE OF ACTION IN THAT REFERENCE PHOTO. DON'T HURRY AND JUST ENJOY THE PROCESS. THERE IS NO RIGHT OR WRONG.

3. DEFINE YOUR SHAPE
GUIDES FOLLOWING
THE LINE OF ACTION
THAT YOU FOUND. THEN
START DRAWING.

REMEMBER, THE LINE OF ACTION ALSO APPLIES IN DRAWING THE MALE
CHARACTER! TRY TO LOOK AT MANY ACTION PHOTO REFERENCES AND TRY
TO FIND THE LINE OF ACTION UNTIL YOU GET USED TO IT.

MORE ABOUT LINE OF ACTION (FEMALE)

1. LOOK FOR A
REFERENCE PHOTO.

2. TRY TO FIND THE LINE OF ACTION
FROM THAT REFERENCE PICTURE. DON'T
HURRY AND JUST ENJOY THE PROCESS.
THERE IS NO RIGHT OR WRONG.

3. DEFINE YOUR SHAPE GUIDES FOLLOWING THE LINE OF ACTION THAT YOU FOUND. THEN START DRAWING!

REMEMBER, THE LINE OF ACTION ALSO APPLIES IN DRAWING THE FEMALE CHARACTER! TRY TO LOOK AT A LOT OF ACTION PHOTO REFERENCES AND FIND THEIR LINE OF ACTION UNTIL YOU ARE USED TO IT.

HOW TO DRAW MANGA CLOTHES

AFTER LEARNING ABOUT DRAWING THE BODY, LET US NOW PROCEED WITH ADDING THE CLOTHES.

LET US START WITH THE EASIEST, THE SKIRT.

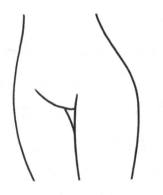

START WITH THE BODY OF YOUR DRAWING. FOR THIS TUTORIAL, I'LL JUST HAVE THE WAIST UP TO THE THIGHS.

THEN, PICTURE THE DESIGN OF YOUR SKIRT AND MAKE THE OUTLINE. BE SURE THAT YOUR SKIRT OUTLINE FLOWS ACCORDING TO THE BODY OF YOUR CHARACTER.

FINALLY, ADD THE DETAILS OF THE SKIRT. YOU CAN EVEN MAKE ADJUSTMENTS ACCORDINGLY.

WHAT IF THE WIND IS BLOWING? HOW DO WE DRAW THE SKIRT? WHAT IF OUR CHARACTER IS MOVING?

START WITH THE BODY OF YOUR DRAWING AND IDENTIFY HOW THE WIND BLOWS OR HOW YOUR CHARACTER MOVES.

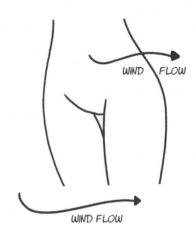

THEN OUTLINE YOUR SKIRT IN THIS CASE THE SKIRT IS BEING BLOWN FROM LEFT TO RIGHT.

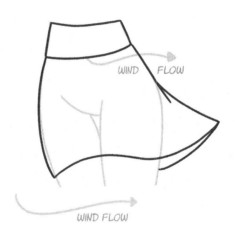

FINALLY, ADD THE DETAILS OF YOUR SKIRT! REMEMBER TO FOLLOW YOUR OUTLINE.

NOW, LET US TRY DRAWING A SHIRT FOR OUR CHARACTER.

START WITH THE BODY OF YOUR DRAWING. YOUR CLOTHES WILL BE BASED ON HOW YOUR CHARACTER'S BODY IS BUILT.

THEN, PICTURE THE DESIGN OF YOUR SKIRT AND DRAW THE OUTLINE. MAKE SURE THAT YOUR SHIRT OUTLINE WILL FLOW ACCORDING TO THE BODY OF YOUR CHARACTER.

FINALLY, ADD THE DETAILS OF THE SHIRT AND ERASE THE BODY LINES UNDER THE SHIRT. FOLDS SHOULD FOLLOW YOUR CHARACTER'S BODY CURVES.

REMEMBER THAT CLOTHES ARE SOFT AND CAN BE CURVED IN ANY WAY FOLLOWING YOUR CHARACTER'S MOVEMENTS.

TIP: TAKE YOUR TIME AND LOOK AT REAL-LIFE REFERENCES AND HOW CLOTHES LOOK WHILE BEING WORN BY DIFFERENT PEOPLE. PRACTICE IS THE KEY! REFERENCES WILL HELP A LOT.

LET US STUDY MORE ABOUT CLOTHES.

START WITH THE BODY OF YOUR DRAWING. YOUR CLOTHES WILL BE BASED ON HOW YOUR CHARACTER'S BODY IS BUILT.

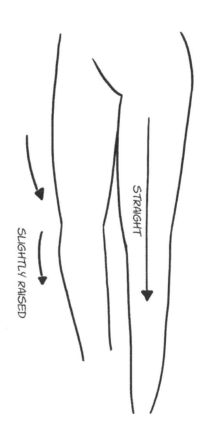

67

FOLLOWING THE BODY, DRAW THE
CLOTHES OVER IT. THIS CAN GET
TRICKY AND CONFUSING SINCE YOU
WILL NEED TO IDENTIFY WHERE
THE "FOLDS" WILL BE. REMEMBER
TO USE REAL-LIFE REFERENCES
AND CHECK HOW THE "FOLDS" GO.

CLOTHES ARE USUALLY PULLED
AND WRINKLED IN THE JOINTS.

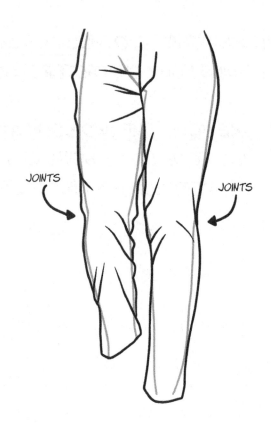

FINALIZE YOUR SKETCH AND ADD
ADDITIONAL DETAILS BY MAKING SOME
LINES THICKER THAN OTHERS.

USING THICKER LINES WILL GIVE
ADDITIONAL DEPTH TO YOUR
DRAWING.

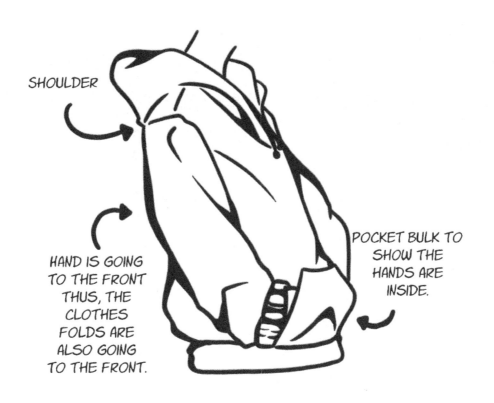

SHOULDER

HAND IS GOING TO THE FRONT THUS, THE CLOTHES FOLDS ARE ALSO GOING TO THE FRONT.

POCKET BULK TO SHOW THE HANDS ARE INSIDE.

EMPHASIZE THAT COLLAR IS GOING TO THE BACK OF THE NECK

SHOULDER

PULLING AT THE BUTTON

TUCKED IN

MORE CLOTHING EXAMPLES.

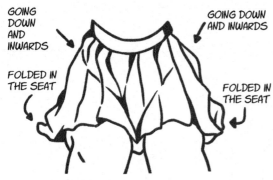

GOING DOWN AND INWARDS

GOING DOWN AND INWARDS

FOLDED IN THE SEAT

FOLDED IN THE SEAT

SITTING DOWN WITH A SKIRT

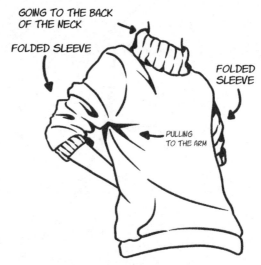

GOING TO THE BACK OF THE NECK

FOLDED SLEEVE

FOLDED SLEEVE

PULLING TO THE ARM

SWEATER WITH ROLLED UP SLEEVES

BREAST AREA

CLOTHES FLOWING TO THE BACK

CLOTHES FLOWING TO THE BACK

TURNING AROUND

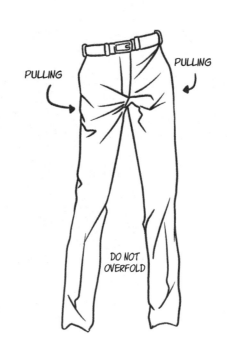

PULLING

PULLING

DO NOT OVERFOLD

GOING TO THE BACK OF THE SHOULDER

PULLING AT THE BREAST PART

LOOSE SHIRT

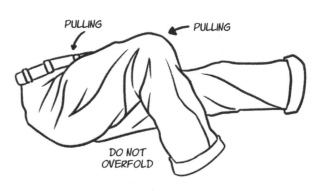

PULLING

PULLING

DO NOT OVERFOLD

DRAWING FINISHED CHARACTERS! (FEMALE)

USING EVERYTHING YOU HAVE LEARNED, TRY TO DRAW YOUR OWN FULL BODY CHARACTER!

DRAW YOUR GUIDES. MAKE SURE TO HAVE YOUR CHARACTER'S POSITION AND MOOD IN MIND SINCE ALL OF THESE THINGS FOLLOW YOUR GUIDES.

OUTLINE YOUR GUIDES. REMEMBER THAT YOU CAN MAKE ADJUSTMENTS TO THE OUTLINE AS YOU SEE FIT. YOUR GUIDES ARE NOT ABSOLUTE; THEY ARE CALLED GUIDES FOR A REASON.

SKETCH YOUR CHARACTER. TAKE NOTE
OF THE MOVEMENT AND MOOD; HAPPY?
SAD OR EXCITED? EXPRESSION,
CLOTHES AND HAIR SHOULD FOLLOW
THE CHARACTER'S MOVEMENTS SO IT
WON'T LOOK STIFF.

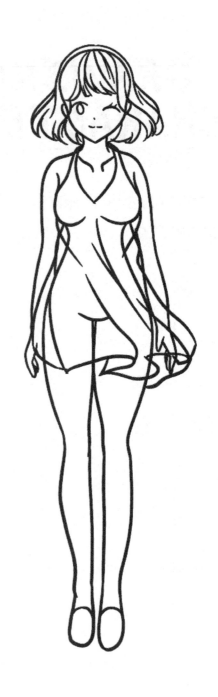

CLEAN UP YOUR SKETCH AND FINALIZE YOUR
LINES. YOU CAN MAKE SOME LINES THICKER
THAN THE OTHERS TO GIVE MORE DEPTH TO
YOUR CHARACTER.

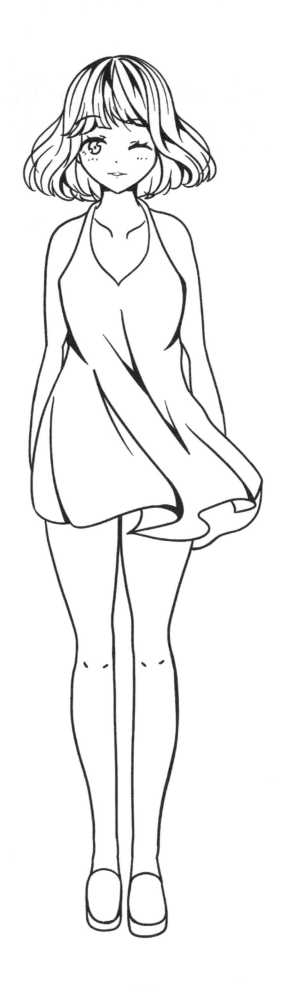

DRAWING FINISHED CHARACTERS! (MALE)

USING EVERYTHING YOU LEARNED TRY TO DRAW YOUR OWN FULL BODY CHARACTER!

DRAW YOUR GUIDES. MAKE SURE YOU HAVE YOUR CHARACTER'S POSITION AND MOOD IN MIND SINCE ALL THE OTHER THINGS WILL FOLLOW YOUR GUIDES.

OUTLINE YOUR GUIDES. REMEMBER THAT YOU CAN MAKE ADJUSTMENTS TO THE OUTLINE AS YOU SEE FIT. YOUR GUIDES ARE NOT ABSOLUTE; THEY ARE CALLED GUIDES FOR A REASON.

SKETCH YOUR CHARACTER. TAKE
NOTE OF HIS MOVEMENT AND MOOD;
HAPPY, SAD, EXCITED? EXPRESSION,
CLOTHES AND HAIR SHOULD FOLLOW
THE CHARACTER'S MOVEMENTS SO IT
DOESN'T LOOK STIFF.

CLEAN YOUR SKETCH AND FINALIZE YOUR LINES.
YOU CAN MAKE SOME LINES THICKER THAN
THE OTHERS TO GIVE MORE DEPTH TO YOUR
CHARACTER.

MORE ABOUT DRAWING FINISHED CHARACTERS!

USING EVERYTHING YOU HAVE LEARNED, TRY TO DRAW YOUR OWN FULL-BODY CHARACTER!

IDENTIFY THE LINE OF ACTION AND FOLLOW IT TO CREATE YOUR GUIDES.

OUTLINE YOUR GUIDES AND MAKE ADJUSTMENTS AS NECESSARY.

START SKETCHING THE ACTUAL CHARACTER, HAIR AND CLOTHES. REMEMBER TO NOT PUT TOO MANY FOLDS IN THE CLOTHES.

FINALIZE YOUR SKETCH AND ADD ADDITIONAL DETAILS AND THICKER LINES FOR MORE DEPTH.

DO NOT BE AFRAID OF DRAWING! DON'T BE AFRAID OF GETTING STUCK AT SOME POINT. EVERY ARTIST STARTED DRAWING STICK FIGURES BEFORE THEY GOT TO WHERE THEY ARE NOW.

ALWAYS REMEMBER THAT DRAWING IS A CONTINUOUS PROCESS. YOU WILL SURELY GET THERE. TAKE IT SLOW. TAKE ALL THE TIME THAT YOU NEED. PRACTICE IS THE ULTIMATE KEY! IT NEVER LETS YOU DOWN.

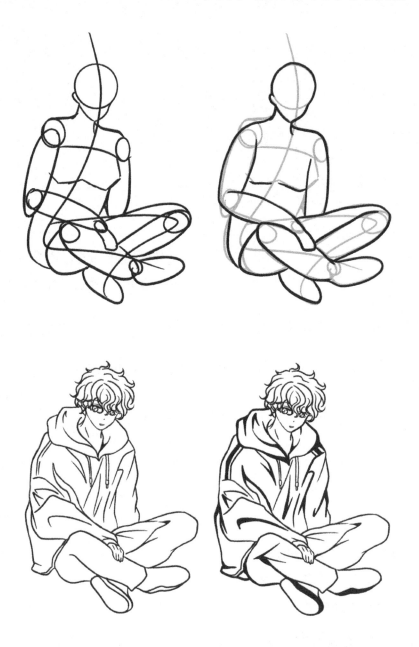

HOW TO DRAW MANGA POSES

LET US DRAW DIFFERENT MANGA CHARACTER POSES!

START WITH YOUR LINE OF ACTION. SINCE WE ARE DRAWING A SITTING-DOWN CHARACTER, LET'S MAKE OUR LINE OF ACTION BENDING AT THE HIPS AND KNEES.

FOLLOWING THE LINE OF ACTION, START DRAWING YOUR GUIDES. WE WILL ALSO MAKE THE CHARACTER LEANING A BIT TOWARD THE SIDE. THIS TYPE OF CHARACTER DRAWING IS CALLED A 3/4 VIEW, A POSE THAT IS NOT A FRONT VIEW AND NOT TOTALLY A SIDE VIEW OF A CHARACTER.

NOW, TRACE YOUR GUIDES. YOU CAN ALSO MAKE ADJUSTMENTS AS YOU GO OVER THIS STEP. DO NOT FORGET THAT A FEMALE CHARACTER IS "CURVY."
YOU CAN ALSO MAKE THE BREAST AND HIP AREA BIGGER OR SMALLER DEPENDING ON THE BODY TYPE THAT YOU ARE GOING FOR.

FINALLY, ADD YOUR CHARACTER'S
CLOTHES. SINCE WE HAVEN'T DONE
A CHARACTER WITH A DRESS, LET
US MAKE THIS CHARACTER WEAR
A DRESS. THIS WILL ALSO HELP
YOU PRACTICE DRAWING CLOTHING
FOLDS.

LET US DRAW DIFFERENT MANGA CHARACTER POSES!

LAST STEP IS TO ADD THE DETAILS INTO OUR CHARACTER! MAKING SOME
LINES THICKER THAN THE OTHER LINES WILL GIVE MORE DEPTH TO OUR
CHARACTER.

TAKE NOTE OF HOW
HER DRESS FOLDS;
THIS DOESN'T JUST
FOLLOW HER BODY
BUT ALSO THE SEAT
SINCE SHE IS SITTING
DOWN.

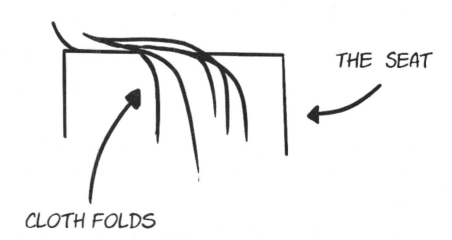

THE SEAT

CLOTH FOLDS

NEVER STOP LOOKING AT REFERENCES TO FAMILIARIZE YOURSELF WITH HOW CLOTHES FLOW AND FOLD. REFERENCES WILL BE YOUR BEST FRIEND WHEN LEARNING HOW TO DRAW.

LET US DRAW ANOTHER MANGA CHARACTER POSE!

START WITH
YOUR LINE OF
ACTION. NOW, WE
WILL DO THE
BACK SIDE OF
OUR CHARACTER.

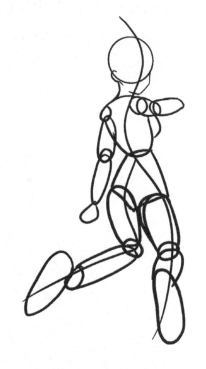

FOLLOWING THE LINE OF ACTION,
START DRAWING YOUR GUIDES.
YOU CAN GO BACK TO OUR
PREVIOUS LESSONS ABOUT THE
TORSO AS A REFRESHER ON
HOW TO DRAW THE BACK SIDE
OF A TORSO.

NOW, LET US START TRACING OUR GUIDES!

SINCE OUR CHARACTER'S BODY IS FACING
BACKWARD, HER HEAD WILL BE AT A $^3/_4$ VIEW
TO MAKE OUR ANATOMY EVEN; NO ONE CAN
ROTATE THEIR HEAD 180 DEGREES.

FINALLY, ADD YOUR CHARACTER'S
CLOTHES. LET US MAKE HER
WEAR SOME TRADITIONAL
CLOTHING WITH A MODERN
TOUCH.

FINALLY, ADD DETAILS TO YOUR
CHARACTER. IN THIS PART,
YOU CAN ADD DESIGNS TO
THE CLOTHES OR ADDITIONAL
STRANDS OF HAIR. YOU MAY
ALSO CORRECT AREAS THAT YOU
THINK LOOK WEIRD IN TERMS OF
ANATOMY.

REST YOUR EYES AWAY FROM
YOUR DRAWING. WAIT A WHILE,
LOOK AT IT AGAIN AND MAKE
ADJUSTMENTS IF SOMETHING
LOOKS A BIT WEIRD TO YOU.
LOOKING AWAY FROM YOUR
DRAWING HELPS YOU IDENTIFY
WHAT IS WRONG WHEN YOU LOOK
BACK.

HERE'S HOW OUR CHARACTER'S
CLOTHES LOOK IN FULL BACK
VIEW:

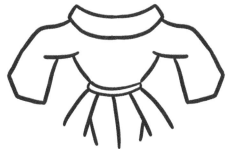

HOW TO DRAW A BASIC FEMALE CHARACTER

LET US DRAW SOME CLASSIC MANGA CHARACTERS WE USUALLY SEE IN ANIME! A FEMALE CHARACTER IN A SCHOOL UNIFORM!

WHEN WE THINK ABOUT THE USUAL CHARACTERS WE SEE IN ANIME, SCHOOL GIRLS ARE SOME OF THE ONES WE THINK OF. START WITH THINKING ABOUT WHAT OR HOW YOUR CHARACTER WILL LOOK. IS SHE STANDING? SITTING? RUNNING?

IN THIS LESSON, WE WILL DRAW A STANDING SCHOOL GIRL. AS WE HAVE LEARNED IN OUR PREVIOUS LESSONS, WE START DRAWING THE SHAPES THAT WILL SERVE AS OUR GUIDE.

START OUTLINING YOUR GUIDES. THIS WILL WORK JUST LIKE IN OUR PREVIOUS LESSON WHEN WE DREW THE BODY PARTS SEPARATELY. THE ONLY DIFFERENCE IS WE ARE DOING THE WHOLE BODY AT ONCE. IF YOU ARE HAVING TROUBLE, YOU CAN DO THIS IN SECTIONS.

IN CONNECTING THE PARTS, REMEMBER
THAT LINE GOES IN WHEN IT GETS TO
THE JOINT AND GOES OUT AFTER THE
JOINT.

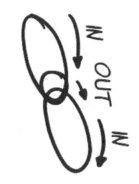

NOW, LET US START DRAWING CLOTHES
OVER OUR SCHOOL GIRL. JUST START
WITH SIMPLE GUIDES THAT WILL
DEFINE THE CLOTHES THAT YOU ARE
GOING FOR. THERE ARE MANY TYPES
OF SCHOOL UNIFORMS (IN-DEPTH
DISCUSSION OF SCHOOL UNIFORMS IN
THE NEXT LESSON).

REMEMBER THAT THE CLOTHES FOLLOW
AND GO OVER YOUR CHARACTER'S BODY.

START CLEANING UP YOUR OUTLINES AND ADD DETAILS AS NECESSARY, LIKE ADDITIONAL STRANDS OF HAIR, CLOTHES, FOLDS, AND CLOTHING DETAILS (BUTTONS, SHADES, ETC.).

TAKE IT EASY AND DO NOT HURRY. ALSO, TRY TO MAKE YOUR LINES LONG, ESPECIALLY IN THE HAIR, LIKE THIS:

SMOOTH LONG LINES ✓

WILL MAKE OUTPUT STIFF ✗

THE SAILOR SCHOOL UNIFORM COMES IN DIFFERENT VERSIONS; THE
SUMMER AND WINTER UNIFORMS.

THE COLLARED SHIRT CAN HAVE LONG OR SHORT SLEEVES. IT CAN ALSO
COME WITH A BLAZER ON TOP OR A SWEATER.

THE PLEATED SKIRT CAN VARY IN LENGTH; IT CAN BE EXTRA-LONG OR
EXTRA SHORT. SOME ARE KNEE LENGTH.

SOME RIBBON TYPES:

YOU CAN EXPERIMENT WITH WHAT RIBBON YOU ARE GOING TO USE ON
YOUR SAILOR UNFORM SINCE RIBBONS COME IN MANY DIFFERENT TYPES!

SOME PLATED SKIRT TYPES:

REMEMBER THAT THE LENGTH OF THE SKIRT CAN BE LONG OR SHORT.

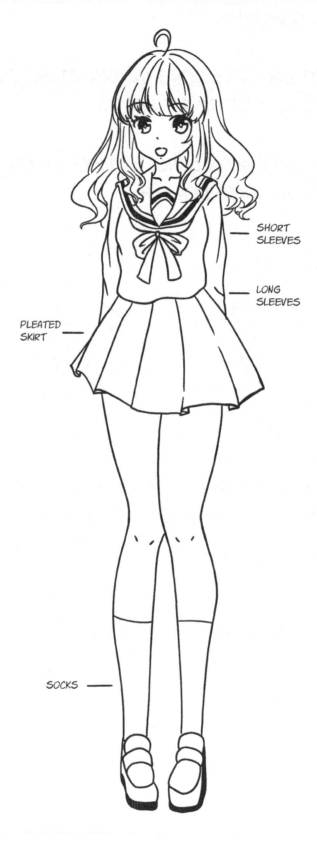

SHORT SLEEVES

LONG SLEEVES

PLEATED SKIRT

SOCKS

HOW TO DRAW A BASIC MALE CHARACTER

LET US DRAW SOME OF THE CLASSIC MANGA CHARACTERS WE USUALLY SEE IN ANIME! A MALE CHARACTER IN A SCHOOL UNIFORM!

LET US TRY TO DO A STANDING MALE CHARACTER IN SCHOOL UNIFORM. AS WE USUALLY DO, WE START BY DRAWING THE SHAPES THAT WILL GUIDE US ALL THE WAY THROUGH THIS DRAWING.

CIRCLES AND LONG OBLONGS WILL BE OUR BEST FRIENDS WHEN DOING THIS.

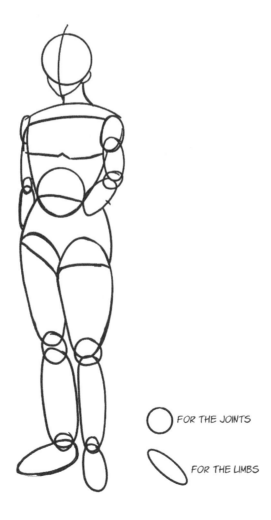

FOR THE JOINTS

FOR THE LIMBS

START TRACING YOUR GUIDES. REMEMBER THAT A MALE CHARACTER IS "BULKIER" THAN A FEMALE CHARACTER. YOU CAN ALSO EXAGGERATE THE MUSCLES DEPENDING ON WHAT TYPE OF CHARACTER YOU WANT HIM TO BE.

IN CONNECTING PARTS, REMEMBER THAT LINE GOES IN WHEN IT GETS TO THE JOINTS AND GOES OUT AFTER THE JOINT.

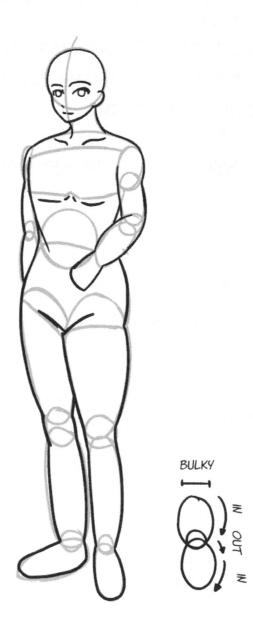

BULKY

IN
OUT
IN

NOW, START PUTTING CLOTHES ON TOP OF YOUR CHARACTER'S BODY. DECIDE ON WHAT TYPE OF SCHOOL UNIFORM YOU WANT HIM TO WEAR (THE NEXT LESSON WILL DISCUSS MORE ABOUT MALE SCHOOL UNIFORMS).

REMEMBER THAT THE CLOTHES SHOULD FOLLOW THE BODY AS THEY GO DIRECTLY ON TOP OF IT.

FROM THE BACK

GOING TO THE BACK

FINALIZE YOUR CHARACTER BY CLEANING UP YOUR LINES AND ADDING NECESSARY DETAILS. HAIR STRANDS, CLOTHING FOLDS, CLOTHING DETAILS AND ADJUSTMENTS TO THE LINES (MAKING SOME LINES THICKER THAN THE OTHERS).

MALE SCHOOL UNIFORM PARTS:
1. BLAZER OR SWEATER
2. WHITE SHIRT OR COLLARED SHIRT
3. PANTS
4. NECK TIE (OPTIONAL)

JUST LIKE THE FEMALE SCHOOL UNIFORM, THE MALE SCHOOL UNIFORM
ALSO COMES IN DIFFERENT TYPES. SOME COME WITH A BLAZER, SOME
ARE JUST THE COLLARED SHIRT
(LONG OR SHORT SLEEVES)

BLAZER   SWEATER / CARDIGAN

THERE ARE ALSO SOME OTHER DESIGNS FOR THE BLAZER AND SWEATER.
TRY TO PLAY WITH DIFFERENT DESIGNS AND LOOK FOR REFERENCES.

BLAZER

HOW TO DRAW CLASSIC MANGA CHARACTERS

LET'S DRAW SOME CLASSIC MANGA CHARACTERS WE USUALLY SEE IN ANIME! A FEMALE CHARACTER IN A MAID'S UNIFORM!

THINK OF A POSE THAT YOU WANT YOUR CHARACTER TO DO.

IN THIS CASE, LET US DO A STANDING MAID CHARACTER.

AS WE LEARNED IN PREVIOUS LESSONS, WE WILL START BY DRAWING THE SHAPES FOR EACH BODY PART THAT WILL SERVE AS OUR GUIDE IN BUILDING OUR MAID CHARACTER.

NOW, FOLLOWING THE GUIDES, OUTLINE THE BODY OF YOUR MAID CHARACTER.

REMEMBER THAT FEMALE CHARACTERS TEND TO BE "CURVY" SO LET US NOT FORGET TO DO SOME EXAGGERATED CURVES. TAKE NOTE OF MY ARROWS AS AN ADDITIONAL GUIDE WHEN YOU DO THIS.

IN CONNECTING PARTS REMEMBER THAT LINE GOES IN WHEN IT GETS TO THE JOINTS AND GOES OUT AFTER THE JOINTS

NOW WE'RE GETTING INTO THE FUN PART! DRAWING THE CLOTHES OF OUR MAID CHARACTER. IF YOU ARE NOT SURE ABOUT HOW A MAID'S OUTFIT LOOKS, TRY TO LOOK AT REFERENCES.

IN OUTLINING THE CLOTHES, YOU DO NOT NEED TO PUT IN SO MANY DETAILS SINCE THIS IS JUST AN OUTLINE AND WILL SERVE AS A GUIDE FOR THE FINAL ARTWORK.

HAIR NATURALLY FALLS DOWN SINCE THERE IS NO MOVEMENT

POINTING TO THE FRONT

POINTING TO THE RIGHT

FINALIZED RUFFLES/ FRILLS

NOW, YOU CAN START CLEANING UP YOUR OUTLINE AND ADDING DETAILS TO THE CHARACTER, LIKE THE FOLDS IN HER CLOTHES.

MAKING SOME LINES THICKER THAN THE OTHERS WILL ALSO HELP IN GIVING THE CHARACTER MORE DEPTH.

ON THE NEXT PAGE, WE WILL DISCUSS MORE ABOUT A MAID'S OUTFIT AND ITS PARTS.

COMMON PARTS OF A MAID'S UNIFORM IN ANIME / MANGA ARE:

1. THE HEAD BAND WITH RUFFLES/FRILLS
2. A LONG FULL DRESS
3. AN APRON
4. RIBBON (ON THE HEADBAND AND BEHIND THE APRON)

NOTE THE DRESS IS NOT NECESSARILY LONG ALL THE TIME; SOME MAID'S UNIFORMS HAVE A SHORT SKIRT. THERE ARE MANY TYPES OF RUFFLES/FRILLS THAT YOU CAN USE, NOT ONLY IN DRAWING MAID'S UNIFORMS BUT ALSO ON THE MANGA OUTFITS.

HERE ARE SOME TIPS ON HOW YOU CAN START DRAWING RUFFLES/FRILLS:

①  DRAW THE GUIDE FOR YOUR RUFFLES/-FRILLS.

②  CONNECT YOUR GUIDE.

③  ADD DETAILS AND FOLDS.

HEAD BAND
W/ RAFFLES

APRON

FULL DRESS

LET US DRAW SOME CLASSIC MANGA CHARACTERS WE USUALLY SEE IN ANIME!

THE MALE CHARACTER IN A KIMONO.

A MALE CHARACTER WEARING A KIMONO! NOW, THINK OF A POSE THAT YOU WANT YOUR CHARACTER TO DO. IN THIS LESSON, LET US DO A "WALKING" CHARACTER. START DRAWING YOUR SHAPES; THIS WILL BE OUR GUIDE WHEN FINISHING THIS DRAWING. SINCE OUR CHARACTER IS WALKING, NOTICE HOW THE GUIDES FOR BOTH FEET ARE PLACED.

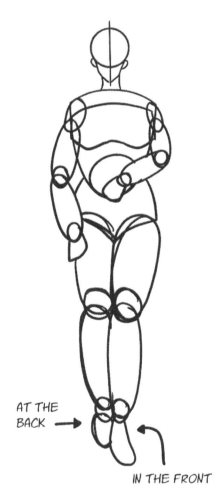

AT THE BACK →

IN THE FRONT

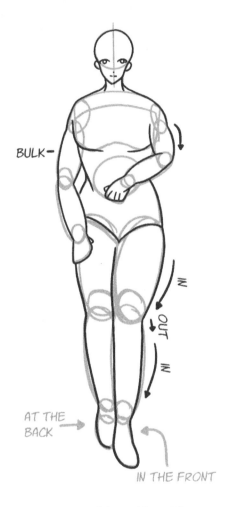

BULK ←

IN

OUT

IN

AT THE BACK →

← IN THE FRONT

IN

OUT

IN

IN CONNECTING PARTS REMEMBER THAT LINE GOES IN WHEN IT GETS TO THE JOINTS AND GOES OUT AFTER THE JOINTS

NOW, FOLLOW YOUR GUIDES AND OUTLINE YOUR CHARACTER. REMEMBER THAT A MALE CHARACTER IS "BULKIER," UNLIKE A FEMALE CHARACTER BEING "CURVY." MALE CHARACTERS TEND TO HAVE MORE DEFINED MUSCLES THAN FEMALES.

START DRAWING YOUR CHARACTER'S KIMONO!

CLOTHES FOLLOW THE BODY AND IT GOES RIGHT ON TOP. SO, REMEMBER THAT YOUR CLOTHES SHOULD BE "FLOWING" ACCORDING TO YOUR CHARACTER'S MOVEMENT.

GOING TO THE BACK

BOTH SWAYING OUT SINCE HE IS WALKING

BOTH SWAYING OUT SINCE HE IS WALKING

CURVED IN FRONT TO SHOW LEFT FOOT IS IN FRONT

FINALLY, CLEAN UP YOUR DRAWING AND ADD IN THE FINAL DETAILS. IN THIS CASE, I MADE SOME OF THE LINES THICKER TO GIVE IT MORE DEPTH. I ALSO ADDED SOME FOLDS IN THE CLOTHES TO EMPHASIZE THE "FLOW" OF THE BODY.

THIS CAN BE TRICKY AT FIRST BUT REFERENCES CAN HELP. TRY TO LOOK AT HOW CLOTHES "FLOW" IN REAL LIFE AND FAMILIARIZE YOURSELF WITH HOW TO DRAW THEM.

WE USUALLY SEE KIMONOS IN FESTIVAL SCENES IN ANIME/MANGA AND THEY
ACTUALLY COME IN DIFFERENT PARTS!

1. HAORI
2. NAGAGI ONLY OR WITH HAKAMA
3. TABI SOCKS
4. GETA
5. OBI

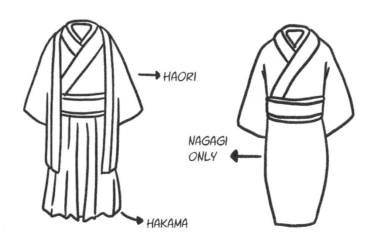

HAORI

NAGAGI
ONLY

HAKAMA

THIS IS HOW A HAORI LOOKS. REMEMBER THAT YOU CAN ACTUALLY DRAW
THE HAORI WITH A LONGER SLEEVE, JUST LIKE THE FULL-BODY DRAWING
WE HAVE ON THE RIGHT.

SLEEVE LENGHT CAN VARY

CAN ALSO
BE LONGER

HOW TO DRAW FUN AND UNIQUE CHARACTERS

NEKOMIMI! CAT-EARED CHARACTER

ANOTHER UNIQUE THING THAT WE SEE IN MANGA ARE THE CAT-EARED CHARACTERS! OF COURSE, IT ISN'T JUST CAT EARS, BUT MANGA ALSO HAS RABBITS, DOGS, AND ALL OTHER POSSIBILITIES THAT YOU CAN THINK OF.

MALE AND FEMALE CHARACTERS CAN BOTH HAVE CAT-EARS OR SOME OTHER EAR TYPE.

THE WAY THE EAR IS DRAWN CAN ALSO CONVEY A LOT OF DIFFERENT FEELINGS.

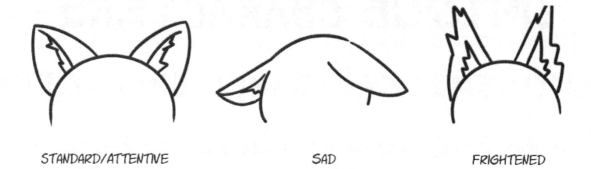

STANDARD/ATTENTIVE   SAD   FRIGHTENED

OTHER ANGLES

ANGEL

START WITH YOUR LINE OF ACTION. THIS TIME, LET US DO A SQUATTING POSITION CHARACTER. OUR LINE OF ACTION WILL BE A BIT SHORTER THIS TIME SINCE OUR CHARACTER IS SQUATTING.

FOLLOWING THE LINE OF ACTION, START DRAWING YOUR GUIDES. NOW LET US MAKE OUR CHARACTER'S HEAD IN THE SIDE VIEW POSITION AND THE BODY IN A 3/4 POSITION. THIS WILL HELP YOU FAMILIARIZE YOURSELF WITH DIFFERENT BODY ANGLES.

NOW, LET US START TRACING OUR GUIDES! WE WILL BE DOING A MALE CHARACTER THIS TIME SO LET US MAKE HIM "BULKIER," NOT CURVY. LET'S ALSO ADD SOME GUIDE SHAPES FOR THE WINGS. NO NEED TO MAKE IT DETAILED; JUST PUT IN THE SHAPES, YOU CAN ADD THE DETAILS LATER.

FINALLY, ADD YOUR CHARACTER'S CLOTHES. YOU CAN NOW ALSO ADD THE DETAILS FOR THE WINGS. JUST FOLLOW YOUR WING SHAPE GUIDES TO MAKE THIS PART EASIER.

LAST STEP IS TO ADD THE DETAILS INTO OUR CHARACTER! MAKING SOME LINES THICKER THAN OTHER LINES WILL GIVE OUR CHARACTER MORE DEPTH. I ALSO ADDED ADDITIONAL DETAILS ON THE WINGS AND SOME STRANDS OF HAIR.

DRAWING THE WINGS!

DRAW YOUR SHAPE GUIDES.

START TRACING YOUR GUIDE.

ADD DETAILS AND REPEAT THE STEPS TO DRAW THE OTHER SIDE OF THE WINGS.

A FEMALE WITCH

START WITH YOUR LINE OF ACTION. THIS WILL DEFINE HOW YOUR CHARACTER'S POSE WILL BE. THIS WILL ALSO BE YOUR GUIDE IN PLACING AND DRAWING YOUR GUIDES.

FOLLOWING THE LINE OF ACTION, START DRAWING YOUR GUIDES. IF YOU STILL HAVE TROUBLE DOING THIS, TRY TO GO BACK TO OUR PREVIOUS LESSON ON DRAWING THE BODY PARTS.

NOW, TRACE YOUR GUIDES. YOU CAN ALSO MAKE ADJUSTMENTS AS YOU GO OVER THIS STEP.

NOTE:
THE FEMALE BODY IS "CURVY," BE SURE NOT TO FORGET TO MAKE EXAGGERATED CURVES.

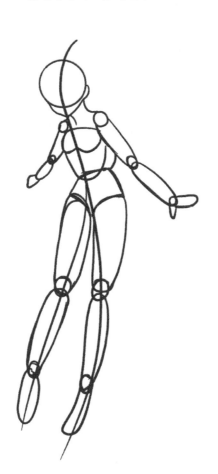

FINALLY, ADD YOUR CHARACTER'S CLOTHES. SINCE WE ARE DOING A WITCH IN THIS EXAMPLE, WE ADD THE HAT AND CLOAK.

MAKE SURE TO LOOK AT REFERENCES IF YOU ARE NOT FAMILIAR WITH WHAT A WITCH LOOKS LIKE.

THE LAST STEP IS TO ADD THE DETAILS TO OUR CHARACTER! MAKING SOME LINES THICKER THAN THE OTHER LINES WILL GIVE MORE DEPTH TO OUR CHARACTER.

ALSO, SINCE THIS IS A MANGA CHARACTER, WE CAN SHADE SOME PARTS OF OUR DRAWING WITH BLACK.

ALWAYS REMEMBER THAT THERE IS NO RIGHT OR WRONG WAY WHEN DRAWING.

YOU CAN ALSO ALWAYS LOOK AT REAL-LIFE REFERENCES TO FAMILIARIZE YOURSELF WITH HOW THINGS WORK, LIKE THE FOLDS OF THE CLOTHES, THE BODY PARTS, OR EVEN THE ANATOMY.

UNDERSTANDING PERSPECTIVES

YOU NOW KNOW HOW TO CREATE YOUR OWN CHARACTER. NOW, LET US LEARN HOW TO DRAW BACKGROUNDS.

BEFORE ANYTHING ELSE, YOU NEED TO UNDERSTAND PERSPECTIVE DRAWING. JUST LIKE IN TAKING PHOTOS, THE ANGLE OF HOW YOU DREW YOUR CHARACTER WILL ALSO AFFECT HOW THE BACKGROUND WOULD BE.

JUST TAKE A LOOK AT THIS SAMPLE; IMAGINE LOOKING AT BUILDINGS DIRECTLY AT EYE LEVEL. THE HEIGHT AND WIDTH OF THE BUILDINGS WILL NOT BE THE SAME AND WILL DEPEND ON HOW FAR THEY ARE FROM YOUR POINT OF VIEW.

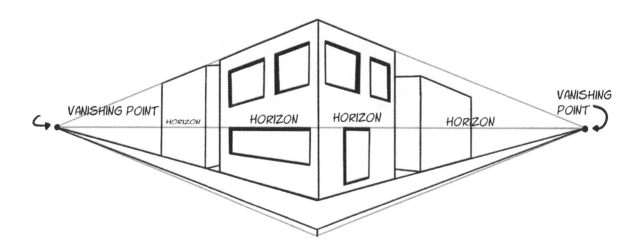

MORE ABOUT VANISHING POINTS:

VANISHING POINTS DEFINE THE PLACE FURTHEST FROM THE VIEWER. TAKE
A LOOK AT THESE EXAMPLES TO BETTER UNDERSTAND HOW A VANISHING
POINT WORKS. REMEMBER THAT THERE ARE MANY OTHER PLACES WHERE
YOU CAN PUT THE VANISHING POINT.

AS FOR THE HORIZONTAL LINES, THEY SHOULD REMAIN PARALLEL TO EACH
OTHER. THERE'S NO RULE ON HOW MUCH LINES OR HOW FAR EACH LINE
SHOULD BE FROM ONE ANOTHER. THIS WILL ALL DEPEND ON THE DRAWING
THAT YOU ARE CURRENTLY DOING.

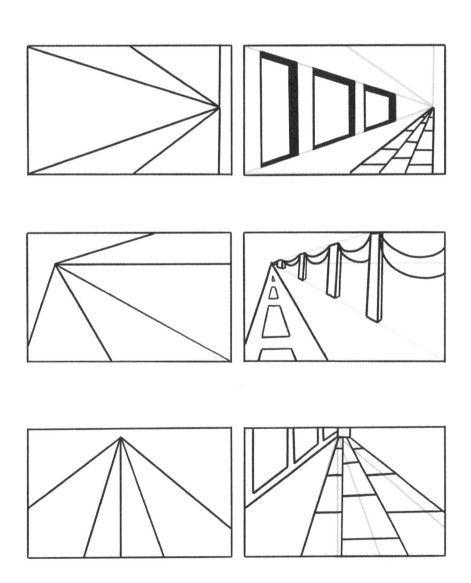

MANGA BACKGROUNDS

MORE ABOUT BACKGROUNDS AND PERSPECTIVES

HAVING TROUBLE WHEN THINKING ABOUT HOW OR WHAT BACKGROUND TO DRAW IS NORMAL.

A TIP FOR YOU IS TO GO OUT AND LOOK FOR PLACES THAT YOU CAN USE AS BACKGROUND REFERENCES. ALSO, BY USING REAL-LIFE REFERENCES, YOU CAN FAMILIARIZE YOURSELF WITH HOW PERSPECTIVES WORK.

IF YOU ARE FAMILIAR WITH MANGA, SOME SCENES AND BACKGROUNDS ARE BASED IN REAL-LIFE PLACES.

THE REAL LIFE REFERENCE.   A SCENE FROM AN ANIME

PHOTO FROM: HTTPS://WWW.CRUNCHYROLL.COM/ANIME-FEATURE/2020/12/07-1/FEA-TURE-ANIME-VS-REAL-LIFE-THE-REAL-WORLD-LOCATIONS-OF-TONIKAWA-OVER-THE-MOON-FOR-YOU

LET US DRAW ANOTHER BACKGROUND USING A REAL-LIFE REFERENCE.
FOLLOW THIS GUIDE:

1. GO OUT AND TAKE SOME PHOTOS OF SCENERY OR PLACES THAT YOU
WANT TO DRAW.

2. LOOK AT THE PHOTO YOU TOOK AND IDENTIFY THE VIEWER'S
PERSPECTIVE.

3. FIND THE VANISHING POINT OF THE PHOTO.

4. START IDENTIFYING THE PARALLEL LINES FROM YOUR VANISHING POINT.

5. START DRAWING THE DETAILS OF YOUR BACKGROUND.

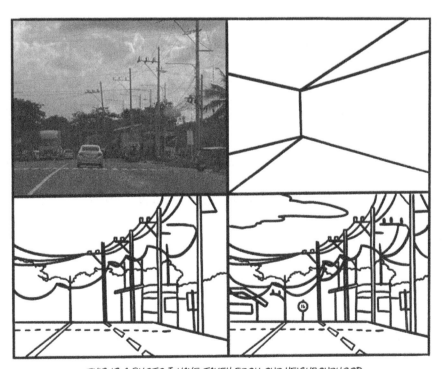

THIS IS A PHOTO I HAVE TAKEN FROM OUR NEIGHBOURHOOD.
TAKE A LOOK AT HOW I CHANGED SOME PARTS OF THE PHOTO WHEN I DREW IT.
YOU DO NOT NEED TO COPY YOUR PHOTO ENTIRELY. JUST USE IT AS REFERENCE TO START
WITH YOUR BACKGROUND.

LET US NOW TRY INCLUDING OUR CHARACTERS IN A BACKGROUND.

LET'S TAKE THE HIGH SCHOOL GIRL WE DID EARLIER AND PUT HER INSIDE THE SCHOOL HALLWAY. SINCE SHE IS DRAWN IN EYE-LEVEL, FRONT VIEW, OUR BACKGROUND'S PERSPECTIVE SHOULD FOLLOW.

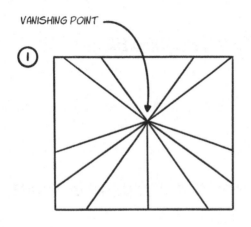

IMPORTANT NOTE:
ALWAYS TAKE NOTE OF THE HEIGHT OF YOUR CHARACTER. MAKE SURE HE/SHE FITS THE HEIGHT OF YOUR BACKGROUND. IN OUR EXAMPLE, OUR SCHOOL GIRL SHOULD NOT BE TALLER THAT THE SCHOOL WINDOWS.

NOW, I ADDED THE HIGH SCHOOL BOY WE DREW. THE REASON HE IS BIGGER IS THAT HE IS MUCH CLOSER TO THE VIEWER THAN THE SCHOOL GIRL.

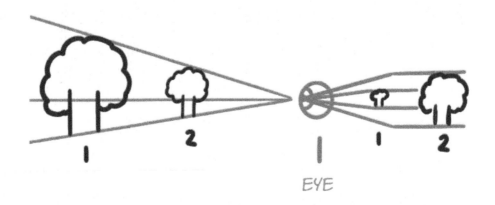

THE CLOSER THE ITEM IS TO THE VIEWER, THE BIGGER IT LOOKS. THE FURTHER AWAY THE ITEM, THE SMALLER IT WILL APPEAR.

MANGA PANELS

CREATING OUR MANGA PAGES

WE NOW KNOW HOW TO DRAW OUR CHARACTERS AND BACKGROUNDS. NOW LET US PUT THEM INTO MANGA PANELS.

1. CREATE YOUR STORY.

BEFORE YOU CAN ACTUALLY PUT IN YOUR DRAWINGS INTO MANGA PANELS, YOU NEED TO IDENTIFY HOW YOUR STORY WILL PROGRESS. KNOW HOW YOUR CHARACTER WILL MOVE.

SCENE 1

HAPPY AND PEACEFUL

→

SCENE 2

SUDDENLY A STRONG WIND BLEW

→

SCENE 3

DUST GOT INTO EYES

→

SCENE 4

THE WIND STOPPED

2. DECIDE ON THE ANGLES PER SCENE.

YOU HAVE TO KNOW HOW YOU WANT EVERY SCENE TO LOOK. IS IT A FULL-BODY SHOT? IS IT A HEADSHOT? IS THE CHARACTER LOOKING UP? WHAT WILL YOU BACKGROUND LOOK LIKE?

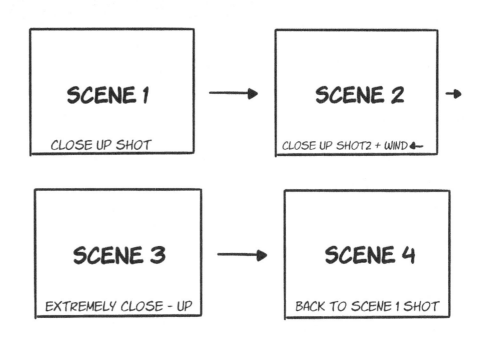

3. DRAW YOUR SCENE.

AFTER CREATING YOUR STORY BOARD, YOU CAN START ILLUSTRATING YOUR STORY WITH PROPER DRAWINGS.

MORE ABOUT CREATING MANGA PANELS

CREATE YOUR STORYLINE AND PACE.

WHEN YOU ARE GOING TO WRITE A MANGA, IT IS IMPORTANT TO FIRST ESTABLISH YOUR STORY. KNOW YOUR PACE AND IDENTIFY HOW EACH OF YOUR MANGA PANELS WILL GO. YOU CAN ALSO DECIDE HOW MANY PANELS AND PAGES YOU WILL USE PER SCENE IN THIS STAGE.

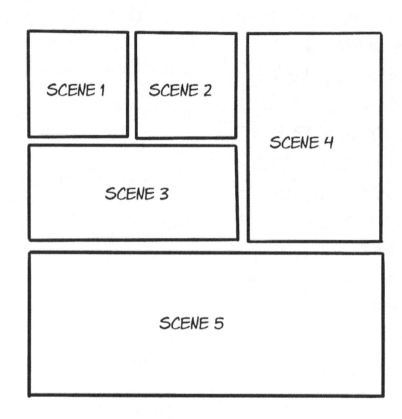

CONSIDER THE READING DIRECTION. JAPANESE MANGA IS TRADITIONALLY READ FROM TOP TO BOTTOM AND RIGHT TO LEFT. BUT YOU DO NOT NEED TO FOLLOW THIS; YOU CAN DECIDE ON THE READING DIRECTION YOU WANT.

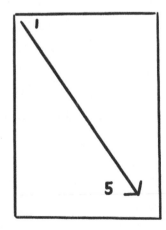
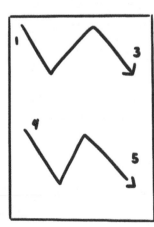
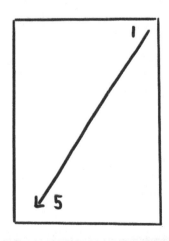

EXPLORE! CREATING MANGA PANELS IS NOT JUST ABOUT SQUARES AND RECTANGLES. YOU CAN ALSO EXPLORE DYNAMIC PANELS. SOME PANELS ARE NOT USED BUT STILL EXIST ON THE PAGE. YOU CAN EVEN MAKE YOUR CHARACTER GO OUTSIDE YOUR SPECIFIED PANEL.

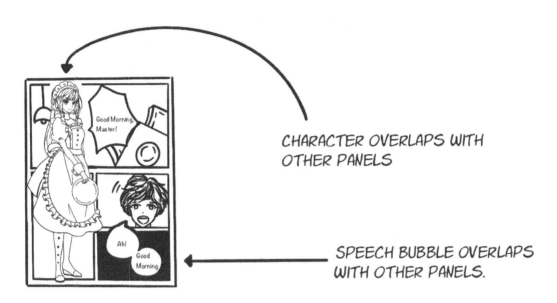

CHARACTER OVERLAPS WITH OTHER PANELS

SPEECH BUBBLE OVERLAPS WITH OTHER PANELS.

GOING FULL PAGE! IN MANGA, ESPECIALLY SHONEN MANGA, THERE ARE ALSO SOME PAGES WITHOUT ANY PANELS DIVIDING THE PAGE. A SCENE MAY TAKE UP A WHOLE PAGE.

FINISHING YOUR MANGA

ANOTHER THING ABOUT CREATING MANGA; HOW TO PUT YOUR SPEECH BUBBLES INTO YOUR PANELS.

1. SPEECH BUBBLES DON'T ALWAYS NEED TO HAVE TAILS.

MANGA DOES NOT RELY ON SPEECH BUBBLE TAILS, RATHER THE SPEECH BUBBLE IS POSITIONED NEAR THE CHARACTER THAT IS SPEAKING (OR SOMETIMES, IT OVERLAPS THE CHARACTER.

2. USE DIFFERENT SHAPES FOR SPEECH BUBBLES.

THE SHAPE OF THE SPEECH BUBBLE CAN BE USED TO FURTHER SHOW HOW THE CHARACTER FEELS. YOU DO NOT NEED TO BE CONFINED TO USING ONLY ONE SHAPE. IT IS NOT JUST CIRCLES AND OBLONGS. BE CREATIVE WITH YOUR SPEECH BUBBLES!

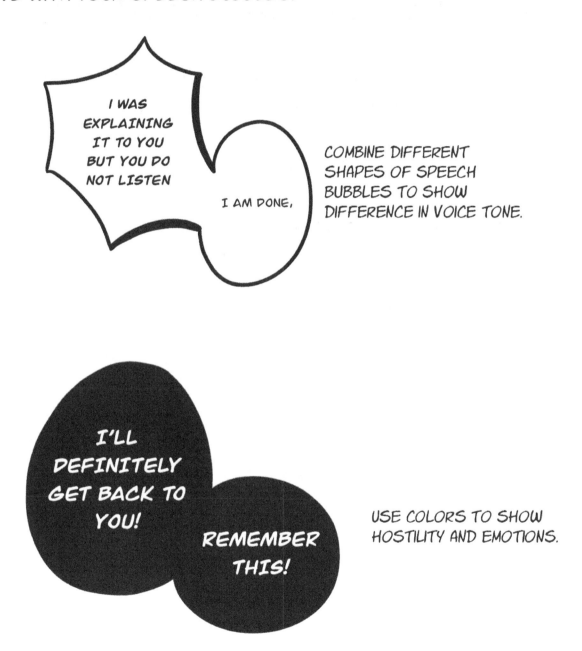

COMBINE DIFFERENT SHAPES OF SPEECH BUBBLES TO SHOW DIFFERENCE IN VOICE TONE.

USE COLORS TO SHOW HOSTILITY AND EMOTIONS.

SUMMARY

FINAL NOTES AND REMINDERS

NOW THAT YOU'VE LEARNED ALL THE BASICS OF DRAWING YOUR VERY OWN MANGA CHARACTERS, DO NOT FORGET TO PRACTICE!

PRACTICE, PRACTICE, AND PRACTICE.

TAKE A COUPLE OF MINUTES AND LOOK AT DIFFERENT PHOTOS OF PEOPLE AND TRY TO IDENTIFY AND DRAW WHERE THEIR LINE OF ACTION IS.

THIS WILL HELP YOU GET USED TO DRAWING SMOOTH LINES AND WILL LESSEN THE "STIFFNESS" OF YOUR HANDS.

NEXT, REMEMBER THAT DRAWING IS ALL ABOUT SHAPES!

TRY TO LOOK AT REFERENCES AND IDENTIFY THE SHAPES THAT YOU CAN USE AS GUIDES WHEN DRAWING.

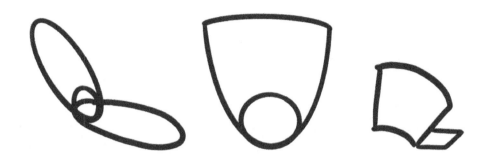

FINALLY, HAVE FUN!

DRAWING AND LEARNING ARE NEVER-ENDING PROCESSES.
DO NOT RUSH!

NO ONE STARTS AS A GENIUS. SOME TAKE MONTHS AND EVEN YEARS. HAVE FUN IN THE PROCESS AND REMEMBER THAT HARD WORK WILL SURELY PAY OFF!

THANK YOU FOR GETTING OUR BOOK!

IF YOU FIND THIS DRAWING BOOK FUN AND USEFUL, WE WOULD BE VERY GRATEFUL IF YOU POST A SHORT REVIEW ON AMAZON! YOUR SUPPORT DOES MAKE A DIFFERENCE, AND WE READ EVERY REVIEW PERSONALLY.

IF YOU WOULD LIKE TO LEAVE A REVIEW, JUST HEAD ON OVER TO THIS BOOK'S AMAZON PAGE AND CLICK "WRITE A CUSTOMER REVIEW."

THANK YOU FOR YOUR SUPPORT!

★ ★ ★ ★ ★

Made in the USA
Las Vegas, NV
29 September 2022

56182377R00072